Reading Social Studies

Strategies for English Language Learners

High Intermediate

New York, New York   Columbus, Ohio   Chicago, Illinois   Peoria, Illinois   Woodland Hills, California

Image Credits: Cover (ship's wheel)Brand X/PunchStock, (globe)Creatas, (others)Getty Images.

The McGraw·Hill Companies

Send all inquiries to:
Glencoe/McGraw-Hill
8787 Orion Place
Columbus, OH 43240-4027

ISBN-13: 978-0-07-874235-4 (Student Edition)
ISBN-10: 0-07-874235-8 (Student Edition)
ISBN-13: 978-0-07-874238-5 (Teacher Edition)
ISBN-10: 0-07-874238-2 (Teacher Edition)

Printed in the United States of America.

1 2 3 4 5 6 7 8 9 10 066 11 10 09 08 07 06

Contents

To the Student

Reading is one of the fastest ways for you to get information. *Reading Social Studies* can help you improve the way you read and understand social studies topics. You will also learn how to improve your test-taking skills.

Before You Read

These steps can help you *preview* an article and get an idea of what it is about.

Read the title. Ask yourself "What can I learn from the title?" and "What do I already know about this subject?"

Read the first sentence or two. The writer wants to catch your attention in the first sentence or two. You may also find out what you are about to learn.

Skim the entire article. Look over the article quickly for words that may help you understand it. Jot down unfamiliar words in your Personal Dictionary. You can ask someone later what they mean.

Participate in class discussions. Your teacher may show you pictures or objects and ask you questions about them. Try to answer the questions.

While You Read

Here are some tips to help you make sense of what you read:

Concentrate. If your mind wanders, remind yourself of what you learned when you previewed the article.

Ask yourself questions. Ask yourself "What does this mean?" or "How can I use this information?"

Look for the topic of each paragraph. Each paragraph has a main idea. The other sentences build on that idea. Find all of the main ideas to understand the entire article.

Refer to the vocabulary you have learned. The words in dark type will remind you of what you learned in the Vocabulary section. For more help, refer to the previous page.

After You Read

The activities in *Reading Social Studies* will help you practice different ways to learn.

A. Organizing Ideas Webs, charts, and tables will help you organize information from the article. Sometimes you will create your own art.

B. Comprehension Skills will help you recall facts and understand ideas.

C. Reading Strategies will suggest ways to make sense of what you read.

D. Expanding Vocabulary will teach you more about the vocabulary you learned before and during reading.

Vocabulary Assessment

After every five lessons, you can try out what you have learned. Activities, such as postcards and advertisements, show you how the vocabulary can be useful and fun in everyday life. Enjoy!

Pronunciation Key

a as in *an* or *cat*

ä as in *father* or *arm*

ā as in *made, say,* or *maid*

e as in *wet* or *sell*

ē as in *he, see, mean, niece,* or *lovely*

i as in *in* or *fit*

ī as in *I, mine, sigh, die,* or *my*

o as in *on* or *not*

ō as in *fold, boat, own,* or *foe*

ô as in *or, oar, naughty, awe,* or *ball*

oo as in *good, would,* or *put*

o͞o as in *roof* or *blue*

oi as in *noise* or *joy*

ou as in *loud* or *now*

u as in *must* or *cover*

ū as in *pure, cue, few,* or *feud*

ur as in *turn, fern, heard, bird,* or *word*

ə as in *awhile, model, second,* or *column*

b as in *big, table,* or *job*

ch as in *chew, much,* or *latch*

d as in *deep, puddle,* or *mad*

f as in *fat, before, beef, stuff, graph,* or *rough*

g as in *give, again,* or *dog*

h as in *hat, whole,* or *ahead*

j as in *jar, enjoy, gentle,* or *badge*

k as in *kitchen, book, mock,* or *cool*

l as in *look, alive, heel, tall,* or *follow*

m as in *me, imagine,* or *seem*

n as in *no, inside, inning,* or *fun*

ng as in *singer, bring,* or *drink*

p as in *put, open,* or *drop*

r as in *run, form,* or *wear*

s as in *socks, herself,* or *miss*

sh as in *should, washing,* or *hash*

t as in *too, enter, mitten,* or *sit*

th as in *think, nothing,* or *tooth*

<u>th</u> as in *there, either,* or *smooth*

v as in *vote, even,* or *love*

w as in *well* or *away*

y as in *yellow* or *canyon*

z as in *zoo, hazy,* or *sizes*

zh as in *seizure, measure,* or *mirage*

Lesson 1 The Blues

Before You Read

Think about what you know. Skim the article on the opposite page. What do you predict the article will be about? Have you ever heard of the blues? What kind of music do you like to listen to?

Vocabulary

The content-area and academic English words below appear in "The Blues." Read the definitions and the example sentences.

Content-Area Words

ballads (bal′ədz) songs that tell stories in many short verses
Example: Many *ballads* tell stories about the ancestors of a group of people.

rhythm (ri<u>th</u>′əm) a pattern of sounds that repeat in an orderly way
Example: When I bang the drum in a slow *rhythm,* it sounds like a heartbeat.

origin (ôr′ə jin) the source that something comes from
Example: The *origin* of the smell was the cake in the oven.

intense (in tens′) very strong
Example: Lakshmi had to make an *intense* effort to move the heavy couch.

wailed (wāld) made a long sound like a cry of sadness or pain
Example: The baby *wailed* when I took the toy away from him.

Academic English

response (ri spons′) an action that occurs because of another action; a reaction
Example: When the doorbell rings, the dog's *response* is to bark.

adapted (ə dapt′əd) changed in order to meet new needs
Example: Latisha *adapted* the spicy recipe by taking out the hot peppers.

Rate each vocabulary word according to the following scale. Write a number next to each content-area and academic English word.

4 I have never seen the word before.
3 I have seen the word but do not know what it means.
2 I know what the word means when I read it.
1 I use the word myself in speaking or writing.

Now skim the article and look for other words that are new to you. Write each new word and its definition in the Personal Dictionary.

While You Read

Tip! **Think about why you read.** Do you know where or how blues music was created? Write down a question about the blues that you would like to know the answer to. As you read, try to find the answer.

The Blues

During the 1800s, African Americans worked long days in the fields of the American South. To make the time go faster, they sang the "field hollers" that they used to sing in Africa. One person sang a line. Then a group of workers repeated it, or sang a **response.** The songs' words told of the hard lives of the people. African Americans also used this call-and-response style when they sang in church. They sang "shout spirituals," or joyous religious songs. They clapped their hands and stomped their feet to the music.

After the Civil War, the music changed a great deal. African American music, which included **ballads** and church music, began to take new forms. It also **adapted** dance music, called "jump-ups," which had great **rhythm.** A stringed instrument called the *banjo,* which is similar to the guitar, became popular. A blues singer usually played a call-and-response with the banjo. He or she sang a line and played a response on the banjo. By the early 1900s, the guitar had replaced the banjo as the main instrument of the blues.

Northern Mississippi, also known as the Delta, was the center of the blues tradition. By the 1920s, the Delta had many blues clubs called "juke joints." African Americans listened and danced to music in these clubs. Some of the greatest blues singers and players performed in them.

Blues have a soulful sound that listeners can easily recognize. The musical notes are often "bent." This means that players change the notes slightly to give a song more strength. Whatever their **origin,** these bent notes most often define the blues.

Lyrics are the words of a song. Blues lyrics describe everyday life. The lyrics are often very **intense** and personal. They tell about sad times and hard work. They describe people who find or lose love, people who have money or wish for more, and people who feel happy or sad and lonely. The lyrics may use humor to describe life's trials and joys. They almost always use the rhythms of everyday speech. A typical blues stanza, or group of lyrics, has three lines. The second line repeats the first line. The third line has different words.

By the 1940s, large numbers of African Americans had left the Delta and moved north to find work. Many settled in Chicago. A new kind of blues, called "electric" or "Chicago" blues, began there. It used many of the same themes as the original blues. However, the new style of blues was played with electric guitars that **"wailed"** and with mouth instruments called *harmonicas*. The music often included a steady, strong drumbeat. The loud, intense Chicago blues was excellent dance music. Chicago blues led to the creation of a new music style: rock and roll.

LANGUAGE CONNECTION

Look at the word *songs'*. The *s* at the end of it makes the noun *song* plural. The ' makes the word possessive. *The songs' words* means "the words of the songs." Find another phrase in the article that contains a possessive word. What does the phrase mean?

CONTENT CONNECTION

Muddy Waters was an American blues musician. People call him "the father of Chicago blues." Who is an important figure in another type of music that you know about?

After You Read

A. Organizing Ideas

What makes the blues special? Complete the web below. In each circle, write down one feature of the blues. Look back at the article to find these features. Some have been done for you.

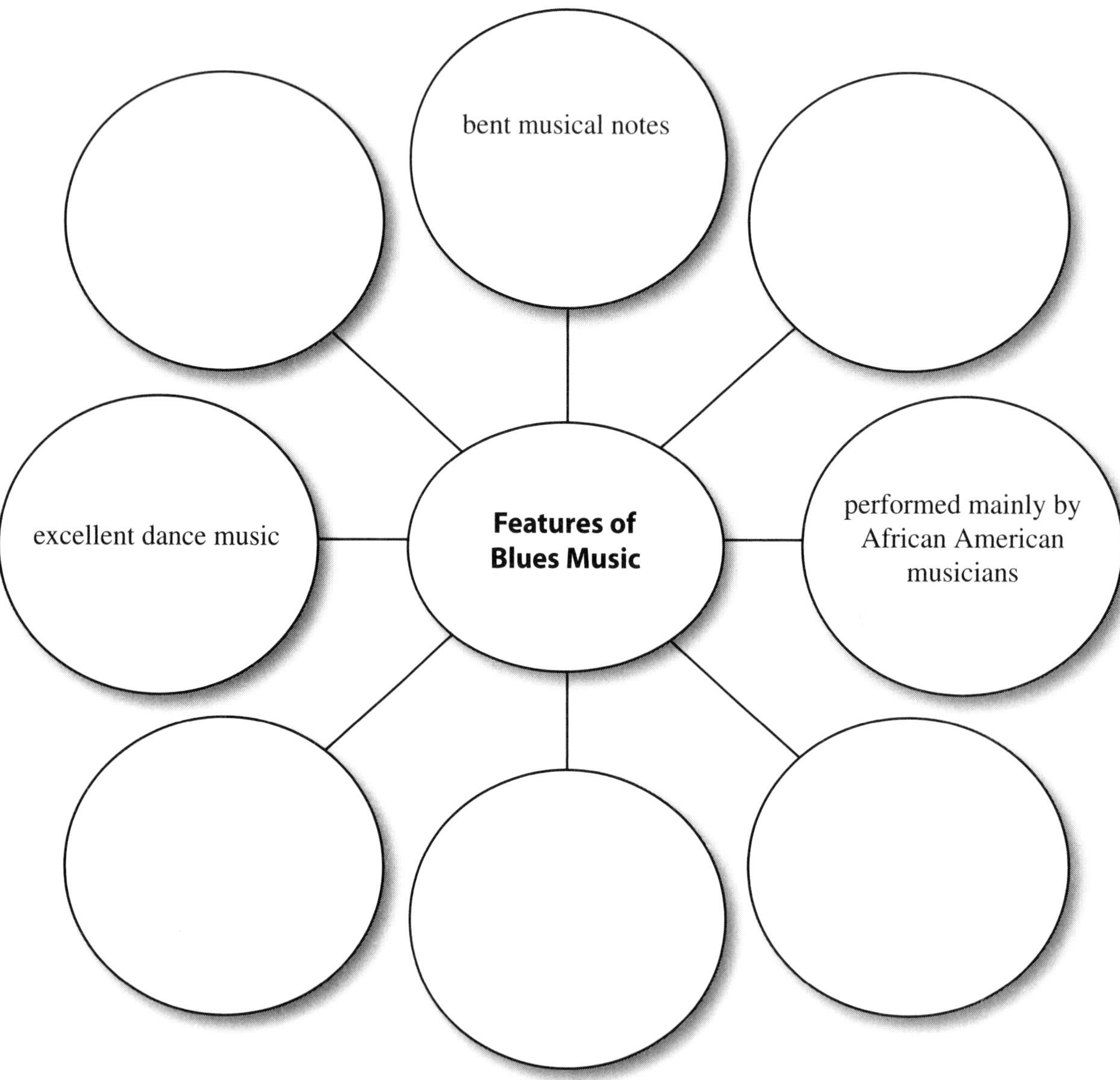

How did completing this web help you better understand the blues? Write two or more sentences to explain what you have learned about the blues. Other than in a web, how else could you have organized the information?

B. Comprehension Skills

 **Think about how to find answers.** Look back at what you read. The words in an answer are usually contained in a single sentence.

Mark box **a, b,** or **c** with an **X** before the choice that best completes each sentence.

Recalling Facts

1. The field holler was a kind of song that came from
- ☐ **a.** Africa.
- ☐ **b.** Chicago.
- ☐ **c.** the American South.

2. Shout spirituals and field hollers both
- ☐ **a.** are sung in church.
- ☐ **b.** are performed with banjos.
- ☐ **c.** use a call-and-response style.

3. A typical blues stanza contains
- ☐ **a.** two lines.
- ☐ **b.** three lines.
- ☐ **c.** four lines.

4. The Delta is located in
- ☐ **a.** Chicago.
- ☐ **b.** West Africa.
- ☐ **c.** northern Mississippi.

5. Chicago blues led to the creation of
- ☐ **a.** rock and roll.
- ☐ **b.** the harmonica.
- ☐ **c.** electric guitars.

Understanding Ideas

1. From the article, you can conclude that blues music
- ☐ **a.** has been successful only in the American South.
- ☐ **b.** became a way to communicate and express feelings.
- ☐ **c.** would not have started without the juke joints of Mississippi.

2. African Americans moved to Chicago probably because
- ☐ **a.** they liked Chicago blues.
- ☐ **b.** more jobs were available there.
- ☐ **c.** the South was too hot in the summer.

3. Compared with the Delta blues style, the Chicago blues style
- ☐ **a.** used more bent notes.
- ☐ **b.** used humor in the lyrics more often.
- ☐ **c.** was louder and used some different instruments.

4. The author of the article would probably agree that
- ☐ **a.** blues music can communicate many human emotions.
- ☐ **b.** blues music focuses only on the sadness of everyday life.
- ☐ **c.** Delta blues music is the only real blues music.

5. From the article, you can conclude that blues music in the United States has spread as a result of
- ☐ **a.** the work of a single musician.
- ☐ **b.** the efforts of many musicians.
- ☐ **c.** several well-known musical families from Africa.

C. Reading Strategies

1. Recognizing Words in Context

Find the word *trials* in the article. One definition below is closest to the meaning of that word. One definition has the opposite or nearly the opposite meaning. The remaining definition has a meaning that has nothing to do with the word. Label the definitions **C** for *closest,* **O** for *opposite* or *nearly opposite,* and **U** for *unrelated.*

_____ **a.** hard circumstances
_____ **b.** easy times
_____ **c.** long events

2. Distinguishing Fact from Opinion

Two of the statements below present *facts,* which can be proved. The other statement is an *opinion,* which expresses someone's thoughts or beliefs. Label the statements **F** for *fact* and **O** for *opinion.*

_____ **a.** Delta blues music is less exciting than Chicago blues.
_____ **b.** The Chicago blues style features harmonicas, electric guitars, and drums.
_____ **c.** The Delta was a popular area for blues musicians to perform in the 1920s.

3. Making Correct Inferences

Two of the statements below are correct *inferences,* or reasonable guesses, that are based on information in the article. The other statement is an incorrect, or faulty, inference. Label the statements **C** for *correct* inference and **I** for *incorrect* inference.

_____ **a.** African American performers have had the most influence on the blues.
_____ **b.** People sing the blues because they are unhappy.
_____ **c.** Blues music has had an effect on other musical styles.

4. Understanding Main Ideas

One of the statements below expresses the main idea of the article. Another statement is too general, or too broad. The other explains only part of the article; it is too narrow. Label the statements **M** for *main idea,* **B** for *too broad,* and **N** for *too narrow.*

_____ **a.** People often use music to express their feelings about life.
_____ **b.** Blues players usually group their lyrics into three-line stanzas.
_____ **c.** Blues music developed from other types of African American music and focuses on the good and bad parts of everyday life.

5. Responding to the Article

Complete the following sentences in your own words:

One of the things I did best while reading "The Blues" was

____

I think that I did this well because _______________________________

____

D. Expanding Vocabulary

Content-Area Words

Complete each sentence with a word from the box. Write the missing word on the line.

ballads	rhythm	origin	intense	wailed

1. The sirens on the police car ________________ as it sped through the streets.
2. The Latin language is the ________________ of several other languages.
3. The book of songs included ________________ about cowboys.
4. My brother has an ________________ fear of spiders.
5. Soraya tapped her foot to the ________________ of the music.

Academic English

In the article "The Blues," you learned that *response* means "an action that occurs because of another action" or "a reaction." *Response* can also mean "an answer that someone gives," as in the following sentence.

When I asked my mom if I was allowed to play soccer, her response was yes.

Complete the sentence below.

1. Shen sent a written *response* to her uncle to tell him that ________________________________

Now use the word *response* in a sentence of your own.

2. ____

____

You also learned that *adapted* means "changed in order to meet new needs." *Adapted* can also mean "changed in order to become used to new circumstances," as in the following sentence.

My younger brother quickly adapted to the schedule at his new school.

Complete the sentence below.

3. When we moved from the mountains to the desert, we *adapted* to ________________________

Now use the word *adapted* in two sentences of your own.

4. ____
5. ____

Share your new sentences with a partner.

Lesson 2

Harvest Festivals Around the World

Before You Read

Think about what you know. Read the first and last sentences of the article on the opposite page. What do you predict the article will be about? What events does your family celebrate throughout the year?

Vocabulary

The content-area and academic English words below appear in "Harvest Festivals Around the World." Read the definitions and the example sentences.

Content-Area Words

festivals (fes′tə vəlz) feasts, parties, or holidays that mark a special event
Example: The town has spring and fall *festivals* each year.

harvest (här′vist) the time when people gather crops that are ready to be eaten
Example: After the *harvest,* the farmer will sell his fresh corn.

excursions (iks kur′zhənz) short trips that people take for fun or for a specific purpose
Example: Of all my *excursions* into the city, I liked the trip to the zoo best.

elaborate (i lab′ər it) very detailed or complicated
Example: Ivan gave his friends *elaborate* directions to his house.

rituals (rich′o͞o əlz) religious or serious ceremonies that follow set rules and patterns
Example: Many cultures have *rituals* to celebrate certain holidays.

Academic English

dispose (dis pōz′) to throw away
Example: The students must *dispose* of their trash in the cans by the door.

devoted (di vō′tid) committed to some purpose
Example: Enrique's afternoons are *devoted* to soccer practice.

Read again the example sentences that follow the content-area and academic English word definitions. With a partner, discuss the meanings of the words and sentences. Then make up a sentence of your own for each word. Your teacher may wish to discuss your new sentences in class.

Now skim the article and look for other words that are new to you. Write each new word and its definition in the Personal Dictionary.

While You Read

Think about why you read. In what parts of the world do you think people celebrate harvest festivals? Write down some guesses. As you read, look to see whether any of your guesses are correct.

Harvest Festivals Around the World

In many parts of the world, people still celebrate **festivals** at the time of the **harvest.** In West Africa, people celebrate the New Yam Festival, called *Iri-ji*. Yams, a kind of sweet potato, are an important food in countries such as Nigeria. In Nigeria the Ibo people have a yam harvest festival each August. The night before the festival, they **dispose** of the last year's yams. A village elder or chief eats the first new yam. Then he offers the harvest to the gods and to the ancestors of the people. Finally, he divides the yams among the people. On festival day, the whole village celebrates. Friends and relatives come to the village to share in the feast. The people eat yams until they feel full. People take part in traditional dances all day and all night.

The people of South India celebrate a festival called *Pongal,* which lasts four days. In this region, heavy rainstorms called *monsoons* come in October and November. These rains water the crops. Farmers harvest the crops in January. On the first day of Pongal, people clean their houses and give thanks for the rains to Indra, ruler of the clouds. On the second day, they say prayers to Surya, the sun god. They offer him a treat made of rice, herbs, sugarcane, and spices. On the third day, the festival of cattle, or cows, takes place. People thank the cows for the work they do to pull plows and give milk. First the people bathe the cattle. Then they decorate the horns of the cattle with colored powder, ribbons, and bells. The cows eat the food that the people prepared for the sun god the day before. The final day of Pongal is **devoted** to outdoor activities and **excursions.** The people also set out rice balls for birds to eat. They believe that this brings good luck and happiness.

Other places also have **elaborate** harvest **rituals.** For example, in Brazil people celebrate *São João,* or Saint John's Day. São João is a midwinter festival, but it takes place on June 24 and 25. (Because Brazil is in the Southern Hemisphere, it is winter there when it is summer in North America.) During São João, people light bonfires to wake up Saint John in heaven so that he can hear their prayers. The festival also involves special foods. People cook desserts made from corn. One such dish, *pamonha,* is sweet corn that is mashed and wrapped in cooked corn husks, or leaves. Another dish, *canjica,* is a corn pudding. Young people wear traditional straw hats and patchwork clothing to look like *matutos,* or farmworkers.

As long as they farm the land, people in these and other places will probably continue to celebrate the harvest.

LANGUAGE CONNECTION

The idiom *take part* means "participate." An idiom is an expression that has a meaning that cannot be figured out from the definitions of each word. Would you rather take part in a soccer game or in a writing contest? Why?

CONTENT CONNECTION

In China people celebrate the Mid-Autumn Festival. This festival celebrates the harvest as well as the unity, or togetherness, of families. Family members spend the day together. What activities do you think they do?

After You Read

A. Organizing Ideas

How are harvest festivals around the world similar and different? Complete the chart below. In the circles, write down facts that apply only to the festival in each circle. In the square, write down facts that apply to all three festivals. Refer to the article for information. Some have been done for you.

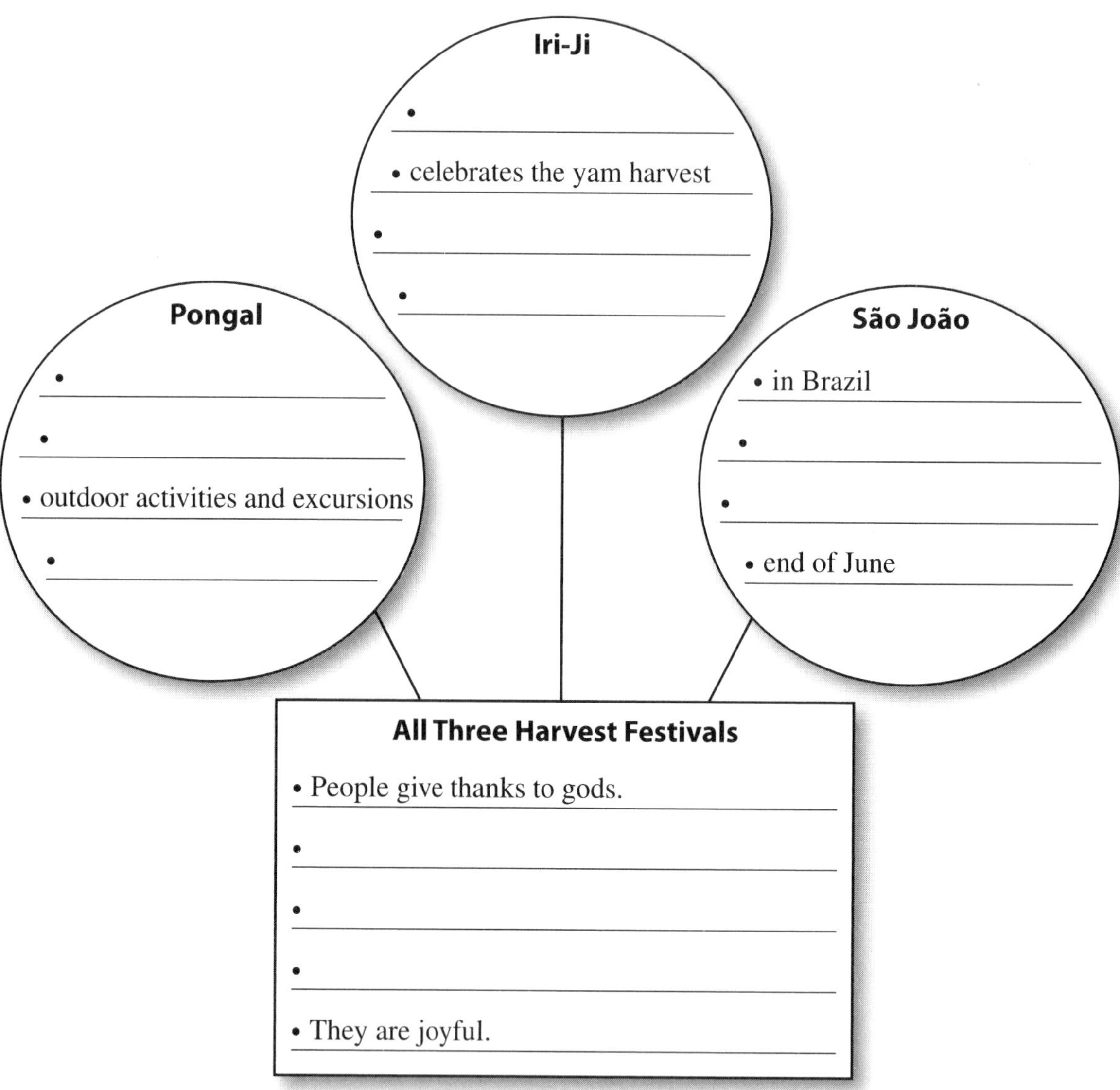

Which festival do you think would be the most exciting one to participate in? Write two or more sentences to explain your answer. How did this chart help you come to your conclusion?

B. Comprehension Skills

 **Think about how to find answers.** Look back at different parts of the text. What facts help you figure out how to complete the sentences?

Mark box **a, b,** or **c** with an **X** before the choice that best completes each sentence.

Recalling Facts

1. The harvest takes place when
- ☐ **a.** people plant crops.
- ☐ **b.** people gather crops.
- ☐ **c.** the New Year begins.

2. A yam is a kind of
- ☐ **a.** cow.
- ☐ **b.** ceremony.
- ☐ **c.** sweet potato.

3. An Ibo chief offers the harvest to the
- ☐ **a.** elders.
- ☐ **b.** gods and ancestors.
- ☐ **c.** guests of the people.

4. During Pongal, people honor cattle because the cattle
- ☐ **a.** will be killed for meat.
- ☐ **b.** help people with farm work.
- ☐ **c.** are good sacrifices to the ancestors.

5. São João takes place
- ☐ **a.** at the end of June.
- ☐ **b.** without traditional foods.
- ☐ **c.** after the monsoons in January.

Understanding Ideas

1. One difference between Pongal and the other two festivals is that the people who celebrate it
- ☐ **a.** give thanks to gods.
- ☐ **b.** give thanks to animals.
- ☐ **c.** do not have a group feast.

2. From the article, you can conclude that people in South India
- ☐ **a.** grow rice.
- ☐ **b.** believe in one god.
- ☐ **c.** value cows more than people.

3. You can also conclude that the Ibo people
- ☐ **a.** do not eat meat.
- ☐ **b.** do not share their yams with others.
- ☐ **c.** believe that their ancestors help the crops grow.

4. The main idea of the article is that
- ☐ **a.** tradition plays an important role in modern society.
- ☐ **b.** people show their thankfulness for successful harvests in many ways.
- ☐ **c.** Nigeria, India, and Brazil are three countries where people celebrate harvest festivals.

5. From the article, you can conclude that São João
- ☐ **a.** is a religious celebration.
- ☐ **b.** is celebrated only when the harvest is good.
- ☐ **c.** involves a week when people do not eat.

C. Reading Strategies

1. Recognizing Words in Context

Find the word *elder* in the article. One definition below is closest to the meaning of that word. One definition has the opposite or nearly the opposite meaning. The remaining definition has a meaning that has nothing to do with the word. Label the definitions **C** for *closest,* **O** for *opposite* or *nearly opposite,* and **U** for *unrelated.*

_____ **a.** older person
_____ **b.** young parent
_____ **c.** child

2. Distinguishing Fact from Opinion

Two of the statements below present *facts,* which can be proved. The other statement is an *opinion,* which expresses someone's thoughts or beliefs. Label the statements **F** for *fact* and **O** for *opinion.*

_____ **a.** The Ibo people should not throw away yams before Iri-ji.
_____ **b.** When it is winter in North America, it is summer in Brazil.
_____ **c.** Some people in India believe in Surya, the sun god.

3. Making Correct Inferences

Two of the statements below are correct *inferences,* or reasonable guesses, that are based on information in the article. The other statement is an incorrect, or faulty, inference. Label the statements **C** for *correct* inference and **I** for *incorrect* inference.

_____ **a.** Harvest festivals are often closely related to religious beliefs.
_____ **b.** In India people believe that cows are gods.
_____ **c.** The Ibo people grow enough yams to last until the next year's harvest.

4. Understanding Main Ideas

One of the statements below expresses the main idea of the article. Another statement is too general, or too broad. The other explains only part of the article; it is too narrow. Label the statements **M** for *main idea,* **B** for *too broad,* and **N** for *too narrow.*

_____ **a.** Around the world, people have different ways to celebrate harvests.
_____ **b.** When people gather crops, it is a happy time.
_____ **c.** Harvest festivals may involve expressions of thanks to gods.

5. Responding to the Article

Complete the following sentence in your own words:
Reading "Harvest Festivals Around the World" made me want to learn more about

____

because _______________________________________

____

D. Expanding Vocabulary

Content-Area Words

Cross out one word in each row that is not related to the word in dark type.

1. festivals	parties	alone	celebrate	thankful
2. harvest	crops	season	gather	hemisphere
3. excursions	corn	trips	travel	visits
4. elaborate	rituals	public	detailed	complicated
5. rituals	rules	patterns	religious	lessons

Academic English

In the article "Harvest Festivals Around the World," you learned that *dispose* means "to throw away." *Dispose* can also mean "to make more likely or willing," as in the following sentence.

I think Dan's interest in books will dispose him to do well in school.

Complete the sentence below.

1. Luk Sun's love of animals may *dispose* him to ____________________

Now use the word *dispose* in a sentence of your own.

2. ____________________

____

You also learned that *devoted* is a verb that means "committed to some purpose." *Devoted* can also be an adjective that means "loyal" or "faithful," as in the following sentence.

I can always trust my devoted friend Neng.

Complete the sentence below.

3. I am a *devoted* fan of ____________________

Now use the word *devoted* in two sentences of your own.

4. ____________________

5. ____________________

Share your new sentences with a partner.

Lesson 3 The Great Seal of the United States

Before You Read

Think about what you know. Read the title and the first sentence of the article on the opposite page. What do you think would be a good symbol for the United States?

Vocabulary

The content-area and academic English words below appear in "The Great Seal of the United States." Read the definitions and the example sentences.

Content-Area Words

seal (sēl) an official stamp or design of a person, group, or government
Example: The college has a *seal* that appears on its official letters.

motto (mot′ō) a short phrase that states an idea or a belief
Example: The national *motto* of Kenya is "Let's work together."

longevity (lon jev′ə tē) length of life or existence
Example: The old man said he owed his *longevity* to his daily exercise.

architects (är′kə tekts′) people who design, draw plans for, or manage building projects
Example: Three *architects* worked together to design the new library.

divine (di vīn′) heavenly; godlike
Example: Rosa said it was a *divine* gift that nobody was hurt in the crash.

Academic English

indicates (in′di kāts′) shows
Example: My high fever *indicates* that my body is trying to fight an illness.

foundations (foun dā′shənz) the lowest parts of a structure that support the other parts
Example: The homes were unsafe because their *foundations* had cracks in them.

Complete the sentences below that contain the content-area and academic English words above. Use the spaces provided. The first one has been done for you.

1. People who want to increase their *longevity* may eat healthful foods.
2. The group of *architects* designed ______________________.
3. Some people express their belief in a *divine* power by ______________________.
4. One group that may have a *motto* is ______________________.
5. *Foundations* are the parts of structures that ______________________.
6. A government *seal* may appear on ______________________.
7. The dark cloud in the sky *indicates* that ______________________.

Now skim the article and look for other words that are new to you. Write each new word and its definition in the Personal Dictionary.

While You Read

Tip! **Think about why you read.** Do you think that one person or many people designe d the Great Seal of the United States? As you read, try to find the answer to this question.

THE GREAT SEAL OF THE UNITED STATES

The Great **Seal** of the United States is a symbol of the nation's principles, or basic beliefs. People began to work on the Great Seal in 1776. The Founders, or the people in the nation's first government, formed a committee to choose a design for the Great Seal. The committee considered several designs before they chose one. Then they changed the design three times before they declared it to be final in 1782.

The Great Seal has two sides. The front side features a bald eagle. This bird lives only in North America. The committee believed that the eagle was a symbol of the highest power and authority. It symbolized the U.S. Congress. The eagle on the seal holds two symbols in its talons, or claws. The eagle's right talons hold an olive branch, which is a symbol of peace. Its left talons hold a bundle, or group, of 13 arrows. The arrows symbolize war, but they also symbolize the power of unity. The number 13 represents the 13 colonies. The bundle **indicates** that united colonies are strong. A shield with 13 red and white stripes covers the body of the eagle. The stripes also represent the 13 colonies. The bald eagle holds a paper that reads *E Pluribus Unum*. This is the **motto** of the United States. It means "Out of many, one."

The front and the back of the seal both show an image called a *glory*. In this image, glory appears as rays of light. On the front, glory breaks through a cloud around stars above the head of the bald eagle. On the back, glory comes from a triangle that has an eye in the center of it.

The back of the seal also includes some other mysterious symbols. The main image is a pyramid that is not complete. The top part of the pyramid is missing. William Barton, the person who designed this image, said that it represents strength and **longevity.** No one knows why Barton left the pyramid unfinished. The great poet Walt Whitman guessed at the symbolism of the incomplete pyramid when he wrote, "The **architects** of these States laid the **foundations**. . . . Now are needed other architects. . . . America is not finished, and perhaps never will be."

A triangle appears above the unfinished pyramid. The "**divine** human eye" is inside the triangle. The person who designed the triangle explained that the eye represents the eye of Providence, or a heavenly guide. It fills the radiant triangle. The Latin words *Annuit Coeptis* appear above the eye. The words mean "Providence has favored our undertakings." Another Latin phrase, *Novus Ordo Seclorum,* appears below the unfinished pyramid. These words mean "A new order of the ages."

CONTENT CONNECTION

Other nations also have symbols. On the Jamaican National Flag, the color black symbolizes hard times, gold symbolizes natural wealth and the beauty of sunlight, and green symbolizes hope and farming resources. What do you think the colors on the U.S. flag represent?

LANGUAGE CONNECTION

Walt Whitman used the word *architects* to refer to the Founders. However, the Founders did not design buildings. They designed the nation by forming its government and laws. What do you think *foundations* means in this sentence?

After You Read

A. Organizing Ideas

What does the Great Seal look like? In the spaces below, draw the front and the back of the Great Seal. Refer to the article for details about the symbols and words that appear on the Great Seal. Label each symbol that you draw.

Front	Back

Which symbol on the Great Seal do you think is the most interesting one? Write two or more sentences to explain what this symbol says about the United States. What other symbols would you have chosen to appear on the Great Seal? Why?

B. Comprehension Skills

Think about how to find answers. Think about what each sentence means. Try to say it to yourself in your own words before you complete it.

Mark box **a, b,** or **c** with an **X** before the choice that best completes each sentence.

Recalling Facts

1. People began to work on the Great Seal
- ☐ **a.** in 1776.
- ☐ **b.** in 1782.
- ☐ **c.** after the Revolutionary War.

2. The symbol of the U.S. Congress is
- ☐ **a.** the dollar bill.
- ☐ **b.** the bald eagle.
- ☐ **c.** an eye in a triangle.

3. The motto of the United States, *E pluribus unum,* means
- ☐ **a.** "Out of many, one."
- ☐ **b.** "America is not finished."
- ☐ **c.** "Glory breaks through a cloud."

4. The main image on the back of the seal is
- ☐ **a.** an olive branch.
- ☐ **b.** an unfinished pyramid.
- ☐ **c.** a shield with 13 stripes.

5. The bundle of arrows that the eagle holds symbolizes
- ☐ **a.** strength in unity.
- ☐ **b.** respect for Native Americans.
- ☐ **c.** the battles that the colonies won.

Understanding Ideas

1. Both sides of the Great Seal show
- ☐ **a.** a glory.
- ☐ **b.** the image of a bald eagle.
- ☐ **c.** the motto *E pluribus unum.*

2. The committee chose the bald eagle as a symbol of the nation because it
- ☐ **a.** is a fierce hunter.
- ☐ **b.** has authority over other birds.
- ☐ **c.** is a powerful bird that lives only in North America.

3. Walt Whitman probably believed that the unfinished pyramid meant that the United States would
- ☐ **a.** break apart someday.
- ☐ **b.** never be a united nation.
- ☐ **c.** continue to develop and change.

4. Barton believed that a pyramid symbolizes strength and longevity probably because the pyramids of Egypt
- ☐ **a.** were built by powerful kings.
- ☐ **b.** have lasted thousands of years.
- ☐ **c.** were built by thousands of workers.

5. The main idea of the article is that the Great Seal
- ☐ **a.** took a long time to design.
- ☐ **b.** contains influences from many foreign countries.
- ☐ **c.** contains symbols of the principles of the United States.

C. Reading Strategies

1. Recognizing Words in Context

Find the word *features* in the article. One definition below is closest to the meaning of that word. One definition has the opposite or nearly the opposite meaning. The remaining definition has a meaning that has nothing to do with the word. Label the definitions **C** for *closest,* **O** for *opposite* or *nearly opposite,* and **U** for *unrelated.*

_____ **a.** hides
_____ **b.** moves
_____ **c.** shows

2. Distinguishing Fact from Opinion

Two of the statements below present *facts,* which can be proved. The other statement is an *opinion,* which expresses someone's thoughts or beliefs. Label the statements **F** for *fact* and **O** for *opinion.*

_____ **a.** The bald eagle on the Great Seal holds symbols in its talons.
_____ **b.** The U.S. motto involves the unity of the nation.
_____ **c.** The Great Seal includes too many different symbols.

3. Making Correct Inferences

Two of the statements below are correct *inferences,* or reasonable guesses, that are based on information in the article. The other statement is an incorrect, or faulty, inference. Label the statements **C** for *correct* inference and **I** for *incorrect* inference.

_____ **a.** The Founders thought that the different people in the United States helped make it a strong nation.
_____ **b.** The people who designed the Great Seal believed that a heavenly being exists.
_____ **c.** Walt Whitman believed that the United States was not ready to be a nation.

4. Understanding Main Ideas

One of the statements below expresses the main idea of the article. Another statement is too general, or too broad. The other explains only part of the article; it is too narrow. Label the statements **M** for *main idea,* **B** for *too broad,* and **N** for *too narrow.*

_____ **a.** The Great Seal has two different sides.
_____ **b.** The Great Seal includes symbols of strength and unity that represent the United States.
_____ **c.** The Great Seal of the United States is an official symbol of the nation.

5. Responding to the Article

Complete the following sentence in your own words:

Before reading "The Great Seal of the United States," I already knew

____

____

D. Expanding Vocabulary

Content-Area Words

Read each item carefully. Write on the line the word or phrase that best completes each sentence.

1. A ________________ may have an official seal.
   city | television | grocery store
2. A motto often involves a ________________.
   sound | principle | color
3. Architects are likely to have a ________________ among their tools.
   metal pot | sewing needle | ruler
4. A person with great longevity has ________________ for a long time.
   worked | gone to school | lived
5. Whenever Marisol wanted divine help, she ________________.
   called the police | prayed to a god | went to a doctor

Academic English

In the article "The Great Seal of the United States," you learned that *indicates* means "shows." *Indicates* can also mean "points out," as in the following sentence.

This sign indicates the path to the lake.

Complete the sentence below.

1. I hope that the tour guide *indicates* ________________________________

Now use the word *indicates* in a sentence of your own.

2. ____

____

You also learned that *foundations* means "the lowest parts of a structure, which support the other parts." *Foundations* can also mean "groups or organizations that give money for research or education," as in the following sentence.

Three nature foundations donated money for a film about tigers in India.

Complete the sentence below.

3. Many education *foundations* give students ________________________________

Now use the word *foundations* in two sentences of your own.

4. ____
5. ____

Share your new sentences with a partner.

Lesson 4 The Ice Age in North America

Before You Read

Think about what you know. Read the lesson title above. What do you think an ice age is? What may North America have looked like during an ice age?

Vocabulary

The content-area and academic English words below appear in "The Ice Age in North America." Read the definitions and the example sentences.

Content-Area Words

climate (klī′mit) the usual weather patterns for an area over time

Example: Animals in a desert *climate* often experience hot temperatures.

debris (də brē′) bits of rock or other material that have been broken up and scattered

Example: Carlos had to sweep the *debris* from the storm off the sidewalk.

peninsula (pə nin′sə lə) an area of land that sticks out from the mainland and is almost completely surrounded by water

Example: Most of Florida is a *peninsula* that sticks out from the rest of the United States.

thrived (thrīvd) existed very successfully

Example: The plants *thrived* in the sunny garden.

extinct (iks tingkt′) no longer in existence

Example: Dinosaurs became *extinct* many years ago.

Academic English

impact (im′pakt) a strong effect

Example: The travel book had an *impact* on which places I decided to visit.

conclusion (kən klo͞o′zhən) a final decision or opinion

Example: Zoe came to the *conclusion* that she liked her new teacher.

Answer the questions below about the content-area and academic English words above. Write your answers in the spaces provided. The first one has been done for you.

1. What word goes with *a pattern of cool, rainy weather?* climate
2. What word goes with *a strong influence?* __________
3. What word goes with *did very well?* __________
4. What word goes with *final thought?* __________
5. What word goes with *died out?* __________
6. What word goes with *land that is nearly surrounded by water?* __________
7. What word goes with *small pieces of rock?* __________

Now skim the article and look for other words that are new to you. Write each new word and its definition in the Personal Dictionary.

While You Read

Tip! **Think about why you read.** What do you want to learn about glaciers and ice ages? Before you read, turn to the next page. Fill in the first two columns of the chart with facts that you know and questions that you have about glaciers and ice ages. As you read, look for answers to your questions.

The Ice Age in North America

An ice age is a long period of time during which sheets of ice cover much of Earth's surface. These sheets of ice are called *glaciers*. Several ice ages have taken place. The first ice age began more than 500 million years ago. The last ice age ended about 10,000 years ago. In North America, it covered the land with a layer of ice 1.2 to 2 miles thick.

Glaciers form when winter snow does not melt completely during the summer. As more snow falls, the old snow underneath it turns into ice. People may think that it is always cold during an ice age. However, the **climate** can be both warm and cold. As the climate changes, the huge sheets of ice begin to melt—and then they freeze again. This causes them to move back and forth.

The moving glaciers pick up sand and other **debris.** They carry the debris with them until they melt in a warmer climate. Then they leave the debris behind, and it forms large hills of clay, stones, or sand. As they move, the heavy glaciers also scrape, or scratch, the ground below them. The melting water of the glaciers fills the gouges, or deep cuts, that the glaciers make as they travel. These gouges then become lakes, bays, and other bodies of water.

People can easily see the **impact** that ice-age glaciers have had on North America. When glaciers scraped away tons of soil in the area that is now Michigan, they formed the gouges that became the Great Lakes. Niagara Falls is also one of the amazing landmarks that glaciers made. Glaciers even had an impact on regions that were never actually covered by ice. For example, glacial ice never reached the Delaware **Peninsula.** However, ice melted from other places and flooded a valley that became Delaware Bay.

Glaciers and ice ages influenced animals too. In the extreme cold, large furry creatures such as woolly mammoths (animals that looked like elephants) developed. The largest animals survived longest. Most animals died out. The animal kingdom continued to change whenever the climate grew warmer and the glaciers began to melt. Some of the animals that **thrived** in the cold became **extinct** in the warmer weather.

At some time during this period, our human ancestors appeared. Scientists came to this **conclusion** because they discovered early tools from this period. As the last glacial waters went down, the first human civilizations began.

Scientists think that Earth is now in a warm period between ice ages. Some scientists believe that the next ice age will arrive about 23,000 years from now. Others say it may begin just 1,000 years from now.

LANGUAGE CONNECTION

Antonyms are words that have opposite meanings. The antonym of the word *warm* is *cold*. Try to find two other pairs of antonyms in the article. Hint: Look for the antonyms of *melt* and *survived*.

CONTENT CONNECTION

People have found frozen woolly mammoths in the northern parts of Russia. Some scientists believe that they can use these dead mammoths to clone, or create, new mammoths. Do you think scientists should try to clone mammoths? Why or why not?

After You Read

A. Organizing Ideas

What do you know or want to know about glaciers and ice ages? Complete the chart below. List four facts that you already know about glaciers and ice ages, and four things that you want to learn about. After you read, list four facts that you learned from the article.

Glaciers and Ice Ages

What I Know	What I Want to Know	What I Have Learned

As you completed this chart, did you learn more about something that you already knew? Write two or more sentences about something new that you have learned about glaciers and ice ages. How could you use this type of chart again?

____

____

____

____

____

B. Comprehension Skills

 **Think about how to find answers.** Look back at what you read. The information is in the text, but you may have to look in several sentences to find it.

Mark box **a, b,** or **c** with an **X** before the choice that best completes each sentence.

Recalling Facts

1. The last ice age ended about
- ☐ **a.** 10,000 years ago.
- ☐ **b.** 10 million years ago.
- ☐ **c.** 500 million years ago.

2. Glaciers form because
- ☐ **a.** the land is very low.
- ☐ **b.** sheets of water cover Earth's surface and freeze.
- ☐ **c.** winter snow does not melt completely, and it builds up.

3. Melting glacial waters fill gouges to create
- ☐ **a.** puddles.
- ☐ **b.** new oceans.
- ☐ **c.** lakes and bays.

4. An extremely cold climate is a good environment for
- ☐ **a.** all mammals.
- ☐ **b.** woolly mammoths.
- ☐ **c.** small insects.

5. During cold periods in the ice ages,
- ☐ **a.** animals thrived but human beings did not.
- ☐ **b.** furry animals grew smaller and human beings grew larger.
- ☐ **c.** large, furry animals developed while other animals died out.

Understanding Ideas

1. Early humans probably
- ☐ **a.** were able to survive in a cold climate.
- ☐ **b.** had very advanced civilizations.
- ☐ **c.** did not know how to use tools.

2. Glaciers have affected
- ☐ **a.** every area on Earth.
- ☐ **b.** large areas of North America.
- ☐ **c.** only the midwestern United States.

3. From the article, you can conclude that
- ☐ **a.** Earth is not likely to have another ice age.
- ☐ **b.** human civilization will not survive a new ice age.
- ☐ **c.** some animals may become extinct because of climate changes.

4. You can also conclude that ice age climates
- ☐ **a.** may vary.
- ☐ **b.** are windy.
- ☐ **c.** are always cold.

5. The main idea of the article is that
- ☐ **a.** long periods called ice ages are part of Earth's history.
- ☐ **b.** glaciers and ice ages have had an impact on North America.
- ☐ **c.** the most recent ice age covered North America with a layer of ice.

C. Reading Strategies

1. Recognizing Words in Context

Find the word *influenced* in the article. One definition below is closest to the meaning of that word. One definition has the opposite or nearly the opposite meaning. The remaining definition has a meaning that has nothing to do with the word. Label the definitions **C** for *closest,* **O** for *opposite* or *nearly opposite,* and **U** for *unrelated.*

_____ **a.** had no effect on
_____ **b.** affected
_____ **c.** collected

2. Distinguishing Fact from Opinion

Two of the statements below present *facts,* which can be proved. The other statement is an *opinion,* which expresses someone's thoughts or beliefs. Label the statements **F** for *fact* and **O** for *opinion.*

_____ **a.** It would be exciting to live during an ice age.
_____ **b.** Glaciers formed the Great Lakes and Niagara Falls.
_____ **c.** The climate is not always cold during an ice age.

3. Making Correct Inferences

Two of the statements below are correct *inferences,* or reasonable guesses, that are based on information in the article. The other statement is an incorrect, or faulty, inference. Label the statements **C** for *correct* inference and **I** for *incorrect* inference.

_____ **a.** Glaciers release a great deal of water as they melt.
_____ **b.** People who are alive today probably will not see the next ice age.
_____ **c.** Ice ages begin and end suddenly.

4. Understanding Main Ideas

One of the statements below expresses the main idea of the article. Another statement is too general, or too broad. The other explains only part of the article; it is too narrow. Label the statements **M** for *main idea,* **B** for *too broad,* and **N** for *too narrow.*

_____ **a.** Ice ages have helped shape the way North America looks today.
_____ **b.** Several ice ages have taken place during Earth's history.
_____ **c.** The first human civilizations may have begun as the last ice age ended.

5. Responding to the Article

Complete the following sentence in your own words:
What interested me most in "The Ice Age in North America" was

____

____

D. Expanding Vocabulary

Content-Area Words

Complete each analogy with a word from the box. Write in the missing word.

climate	debris	peninsula	thrived	extinct

1. mountain : large :: ____________________ : small
2. gone : here :: ____________________ : alive
3. strong : weak :: ____________________ : died
4. population : people :: ____________________ : weather
5. finger : hand :: ____________________ : mainland

Academic English

In the article "The Ice Age in North America," you learned that *impact* means "a strong effect." *Impact* can also mean "the action of one object as it hits another," as in the following sentence.

The speeding car hit the car in front of it with a great impact.

Complete the sentence below.

1. I could hear the *impact* when the falling tree ____

Now use the word *impact* in a sentence of your own.

2. ____

   ____

You also learned that *conclusion* means "a final decision or opinion." *Conclusion* can also mean "the end of an event," as in the following sentence.

The crowd began to clap at the conclusion of the president's speech.

Complete the sentence below.

3. At the *conclusion* of the school year, we will ____

Now use the word *conclusion* in two sentences of your own.

4. ____
5. ____

Share your new sentences with a partner.

Lesson 5

The Social Impact of Television

Before You Read

Think about what you know. Read the lesson title above. What kinds of television shows do you watch? Do you think that they have an impact on you?

Vocabulary

The content-area and academic English words below appear in "The Social Impact of Television." Read the definitions and the example sentences.

Content-Area Words

critics (krit′iks) people who disapprove of or find fault with something
Example: *Critics* of the new train station say that not enough people use it.

sponsor (spon′sər) a person or group that pays for an event or a program
Example: We asked the bank to be the *sponsor* for the music festival.

candidates (kan′də dāts′) people who try to win an office or honor
Example: Lee Ann is one of the *candidates* for class president.

controversy (kon′trə vur′sē) a disagreement that involves different opinions
Example: The tied baseball game created *controversy* among the students.

stereotype (ster′ē ə tīp′) to present a person or group in an overly simple way based on how people believe that person or group usually acts
Example: Many people *stereotype* all nurses as women.

Academic English

positive (poz′ə tiv) helpful; good
Example: Exercise has a *positive* effect on a person's health.

minority (mə nôr′ə tē) a racial, religious, political, or other group that is different from the larger group it is a part of
Example: Native Americans are a *minority* group in the United States.

Do any of the words above seem related? Sort the seven vocabulary words into two or more categories. Write the words down on note cards or in a chart. Words may fit into more than one group. You may wish to work with a partner for this activity.

Now skim the article and look for other words that are new to you. Write each new word and its definition in the Personal Dictionary.

While You Read

 **Think about why you read.** Do you think that television is more helpful or more harmful to people? As you read, look for at least two ways that television may help people and two ways that it may harm people.

The Social Impact of Television

Television—TV—first became popular in the 1940s. At that time, TV brought people together. People gathered in the home of the lucky neighbor who owned a TV set. TV still has impacts on society. Some of the impacts are **positive,** but some are not.

Today TV often isolates people. In many American homes, each family member has a TV set in his or her bedroom. Each watches his or her own programs. People spend less time with family and friends. Some medical experts believe that TV is bad for a person's health. Many Americans are "couch potatoes." They spend most of their time sitting around and watching TV.

On the positive side, people can get the latest news on TV at any time of the day. They can learn how people live in other parts of the world. This helps people to better understand global problems. Some TV channels bring excellent music, dance, and drama into the home. TV does not always have a serious purpose, though. TV also provides entertainment and escape, which are things that everyone needs and enjoys.

However, some **critics** claim that too much escape can harm TV viewers. Escape may numb, or dull, the mind. Viewers who watch too much TV lose interest in the "real world." The world that people see on TV does not match the real world that they live in. Often TV presents a world that seems perfect. Ads try to sell products that appear on TV to people who cannot afford them. Too often the **sponsor** of a show can control the content, or what takes place, in a show. Sponsors want to appeal to many kinds of people. This often makes the shows less interesting. Few sponsors will take a chance on new, unusual programs.

On the plus side, television is good for democracy. **Candidates** often appear on television to discuss their views before elections. People can watch election results on TV as soon as the results are available. However, political ads are not free. TV channels sell time to candidates. The candidate with the most money may have an unfair advantage, because he or she can buy more ad time.

The content of TV programs often causes **controversy.** For example, programs sometimes **stereotype** people—especially **minority** groups. This may affect the way viewers think about minorities. However, TV violence receives the most criticism. Programmers say that "violence sells." The more violence a show has, the more people watch it. Opponents argue that TV violence is not like real-world violence. Violence on TV rarely has real consequences, or effects. Some experts fear that TV violence may cause people—especially children—to commit violent acts.

LANGUAGE CONNECTION

Do you know what the word *isolates* means? Try to figure out its meaning by looking at the text around it. Write down what you think *isolates* means. Then share your definition with a partner.

CONTENT CONNECTION

American children watch an average of almost 25 hours of TV per week, or 3½ hours per day. Children spend more time watching TV than doing any other activity except sleeping. How many hours of TV do you watch in one day? In one week?

After You Read

A. Organizing Ideas

How does television affect the people who watch it? Complete the chart below. In the first column, list facts about TV. In the second column, write sentences to explain how these facts may affect people who watch TV. Use the article to help you. Some have been done for you.

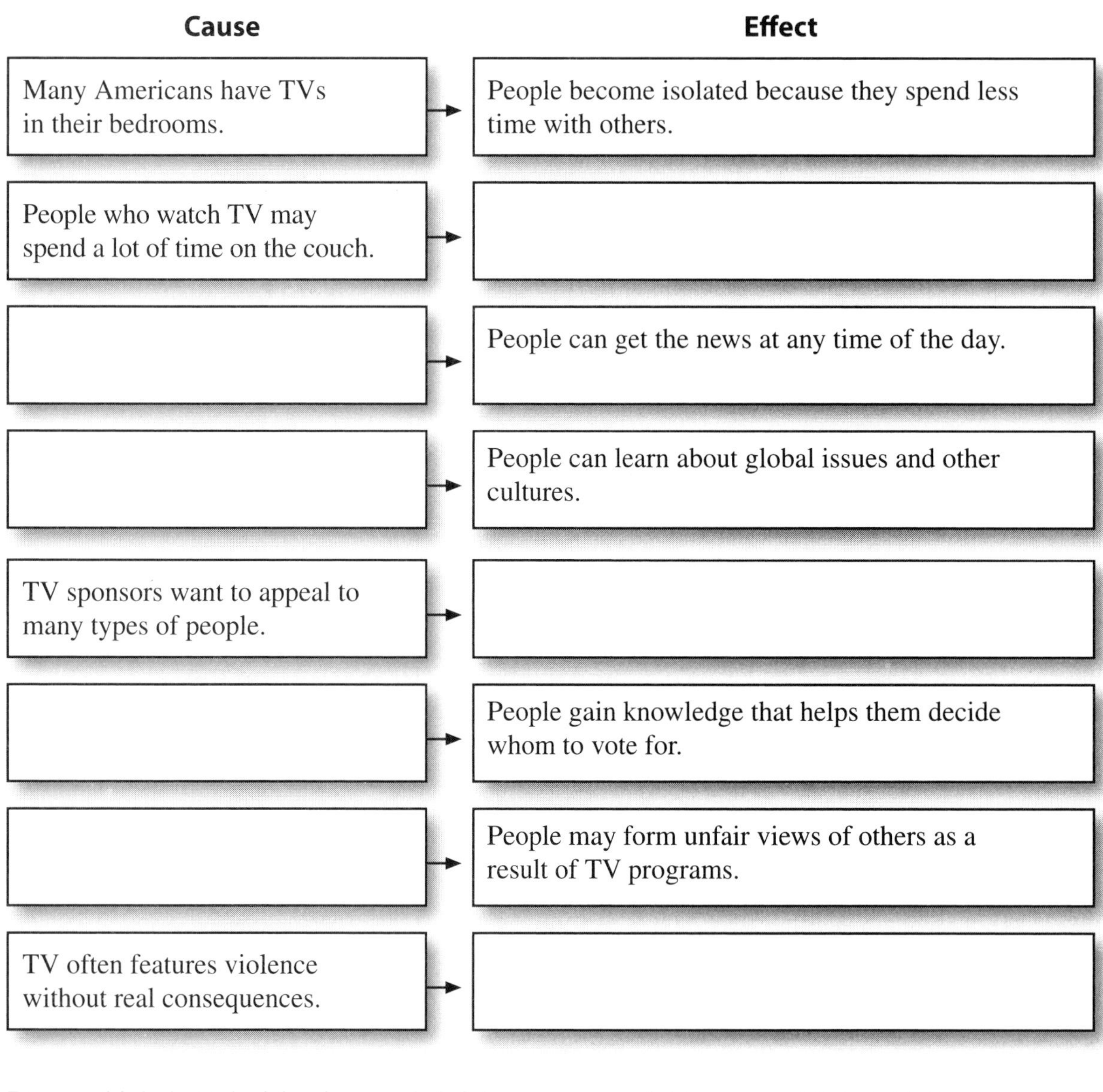

Cause	Effect
Many Americans have TVs in their bedrooms.	People become isolated because they spend less time with others.
People who watch TV may spend a lot of time on the couch.	
	People can get the news at any time of the day.
	People can learn about global issues and other cultures.
TV sponsors want to appeal to many types of people.	
	People gain knowledge that helps them decide whom to vote for.
	People may form unfair views of others as a result of TV programs.
TV often features violence without real consequences.	

Do you think that television is more helpful or more harmful to viewers? Why? Write two or more sentences to explain your answer. How did completing this chart help you come to your conclusion?

B. Comprehension Skills

Tip! **Think about how to find answers.** Read each sentence below. Underline the words that will help you figure out how to complete each item.

Mark box **a, b,** or **c** with an **X** before the choice that best completes each sentence.

Recalling Facts

1. TV first became popular in the
- ☐ **a.** 1940s.
- ☐ **b.** 1950s.
- ☐ **c.** 1970s.

2. One good thing about TV news is that
- ☐ **a.** it provides escape.
- ☐ **b.** it has no commercials.
- ☐ **c.** people may watch it as it takes place.

3. TV violence is different from real-world violence because
- ☐ **a.** nobody gets hurt on TV.
- ☐ **b.** more people are killed on TV.
- ☐ **c.** TV violence rarely has real consequences.

4. TV is good for democracy because political candidates can
- ☐ **a.** show ads for free.
- ☐ **b.** stereotype groups of people.
- ☐ **c.** discuss their views before elections.

5. The content of a TV program is often controlled by
- ☐ **a.** the votes of its viewers.
- ☐ **b.** the sponsor of the show.
- ☐ **c.** events in the real world.

Understanding Ideas

1. Compared with people in the 1940s, people who watch TV today are probably
- ☐ **a.** more social.
- ☐ **b.** more isolated.
- ☐ **c.** less interested in the programs.

2. From the article, you can conclude that most Americans
- ☐ **a.** do not like to watch TV.
- ☐ **b.** watch TV for entertainment and information.
- ☐ **c.** get information about political candidates only through TV.

3. The author of the article would probably agree that TV has had
- ☐ **a.** a bad impact on society.
- ☐ **b** a good impact on society.
- ☐ **c.** both good and bad impacts on society.

4. From the article, you can conclude that
- ☐ **a.** it may be harmful to watch too much TV.
- ☐ **b.** political candidates with the most TV ads always win elections.
- ☐ **c.** the government should pass more laws to control TV programs.

5. The article suggests that TV ads
- ☐ **a.** fail to sell products.
- ☐ **b.** try to influence the way people spend money.
- ☐ **c.** are often more interesting than TV shows.

C. Reading Strategies

1. Recognizing Words in Context

Find the word *appeal* in the article. One definition below is closest to the meaning of that word. One definition has the opposite or nearly the opposite meaning. The remaining definition has a meaning that has nothing to do with the word. Label the definitions **C** for *closest,* **O** for *opposite* or *nearly opposite,* and **U** for *unrelated.*

_____ **a.** to send information to people
_____ **b.** to make people dislike something
_____ **c.** to be interesting to people

2. Distinguishing Fact from Opinion

Two of the statements below present *facts,* which can be proved. The other statement is an *opinion,* which expresses someone's thoughts or beliefs. Label the statements **F** for *fact* and **O** for *opinion.*

_____ **a.** Some medical experts believe that TV is harmful.
_____ **b.** People can watch news on TV at any time of the day.
_____ **c.** A great way to relax is to watch TV.

3. Making Correct Inferences

Two of the statements below are correct *inferences,* or reasonable guesses, that are based on information in the article. The other statement is an incorrect, or faulty, inference. Label the statements **C** for *correct* inference and **I** for *incorrect* inference.

_____ **a.** Some people may want to be more like characters on TV shows.
_____ **b.** People who watch TV are not as smart as people who do not watch TV.
_____ **c.** Stereotypes often do not show people in a positive way.

4. Understanding Main Ideas

One of the statements below expresses the main idea of the article. Another statement is too general, or too broad. The other explains only part of the article; it is too narrow. Label the statements **M** for *main idea,* **B** for *too broad,* and **N** for *too narrow.*

_____ **a.** TV has provided information and entertainment for years.
_____ **b.** The content of TV programs often causes controversy.
_____ **c.** TV may have good and bad effects on the people who watch it.

5. Responding to the Article

Complete the following sentences in your own words:

One of the things I did best while reading "The Social Impact of Television" was

____

I think that I did this well because ____

____

D. Expanding Vocabulary

Content-Area Words

Complete each sentence with a word from the box. Write the missing word on the line.

critics	sponsor	candidates	controversy	stereotype

1. The band's music creates ________________ because the lyrics are often violent.
2. Both ________________ for mayor support helmet laws for people who ride bikes.
3. ________________ of the play said that the actors did not show enough feeling.
4. The race car showed the name of its ________________ on its sides.
5. I think that some people ________________ teenagers as selfish.

Academic English

In the article "The Social Impact of Television," you learned that *positive* means "helpful" or "good." *Positive* can also mean "certain" or "without doubt," as in the following sentence.

I am positive that I put my wallet in the drawer.

Complete the sentence below.

1. The doctor said she was *positive* that ________________________________

Now use the word *positive* in a sentence of your own.

2. ____

____

You also learned that *minority* means "a racial, religious, political, or other group that is different from the larger group it is a part of." *Minority* can also mean "a number or group that makes up less than half of a total," as in the following sentence.

Because a minority of people voted yes to the new law, it was not passed.

Complete the sentence below.

3. Only a *minority* of people who saw the movie ________________________________

Now use the word *minority* in two sentences of your own.

4. ____
5. ____

Share your new sentences with a partner.

Vocabulary Assessment

Writing a Newspaper Article

Read the article. Then complete the sentences. Use words from the Word Bank.

Daily News • Social Studies

Scientists Discover Bones from Ice Age

by Diego Sanchez

Last month scientists in Nevada dug up several large bones. They came to the (1) ________________ that the bones are from a woolly mammoth. Dr. Lin, the leader of the research team, said that some mammals (2) ________________ to survive the cold of ice ages. They (3) ________________ until the (4) ________________ became warmer and the ice ages ended. Then they became extinct. Dr. Lin's team can continue to work for another year because of money from several (5) ________________ that support this type of research.

Word Bank

foundations	adapted
conclusion	climate
thrived	

Reading an Instant-Messaging Conversation

Read the instant-messaging conversation between Rosario and Anna.
Circle the word that completes each sentence.

INSTA-CHAT

Rosario: Hi, Anna! I'm visiting my relatives in Texas. Are you swimming at the lake every day like our other friends?

Anna: No. I guess I am in the (**harvest, minority**). I'm volunteering each week at a farm with horses. We teach young children how to ride horses.

Rosario: That sounds like fun!

Anna: It is. Sometimes the days are long and (**intense, divine**), but it's worth it. The kids love to take (**excursions, ballads**) into the woods.

Rosario: Do the horses obey you and the kids?

Anna: Yes, the horses seem (**elaborate, devoted**) to the kids. It's a (**positive, extinct**) experience for the horses, the kids, and me.

Rosario: Maybe I'll try riding a horse here in Texas! I have to go now. Let's IM soon!

Making Connections

Work with a partner. Talk about what the words mean. How can you use the words to talk about a problem in your community? List your ideas in the outline of the garbage truck below.

response	indicates	impact	architects	dispose
controversy	candidates	critics	motto	debris

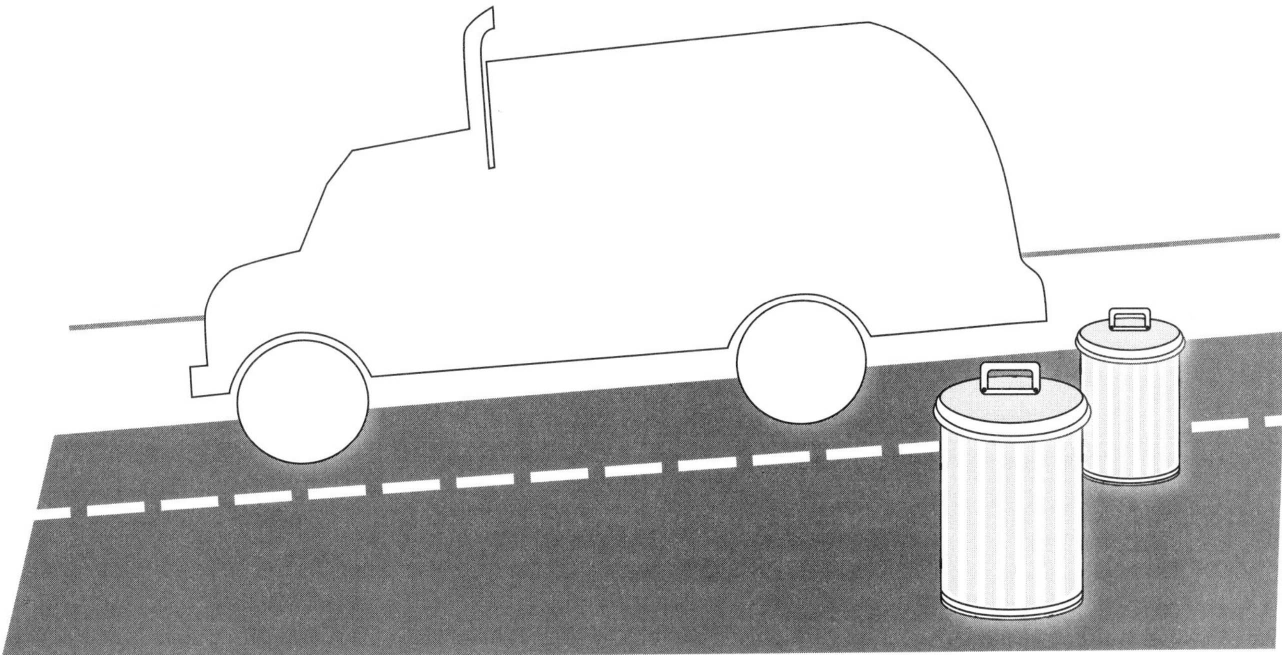

Use all of the words above in a paragraph of your own. Each sentence may include one or more of the words. To help you start writing, look at the ideas you wrote about. After you write your paragraph, read it over. If you find a mistake, correct it.

Lesson 6 King Tutankhamen

Before You Read

Think about what you know. Read the title and the first sentence of the article on the opposite page. Think about what you already know about Egypt. Have you ever heard of King Tut?

Vocabulary

The content-area and academic English words below appear in "King Tutankhamen." Read the definitions and the example sentences.

Content-Area Words

turmoil (tur′moil) confusion that creates unrest

Example: The loud sounds of the fire alarm caused *turmoil* in the lunchroom.

revival (ri vī′vəl) the act of something coming back into existence or use

Example: The clothing designer predicted a *revival* of fashions from 20 years ago.

rumors (ro͞o′mərz) stories that people tell whether or not they are true

Example: Dan heard *rumors* that the teacher planned to quit her job.

archaeologist (är′kē ol′ə jist) a person who digs up and studies the remains of ancient cities to learn how people lived long ago

Example: The *archaeologist* uncovered tools from thousands of years ago.

artifacts (är′tə fakts′) objects made and used by ancient people

Example: At the museum, we saw jewelry and other *artifacts* from ancient Egypt.

Academic English

conflict (kon′flikt) disagreement

Example: The girls were in *conflict* about what movie to see.

retained (ri tānd′) continued to have or hold

Example: When we moved to a new house, we *retained* our old furniture.

Answer the questions below. Circle the part of each question that is the answer. The first one has been done for you.

1. Would a person be more likely to feel *turmoil* about (a new school) or a new bike?
2. Do people in *conflict* argue with each other or encourage each other?
3. Does the *revival* of an idea mean that people rethink it or ignore it?
4. Would someone who has *retained* friends still see them or no longer see them?
5. Would an *archaeologist* predict the future or analyze the past?
6. Do *rumors* involve words or furniture?
7. Which are *artifacts:* pots in a modern kitchen or pots used 2,000 years ago?

Now skim the article and look for other words that are new to you. Write each new word and its definition in the Personal Dictionary.

While You Read

Think about why you read. For how long do you think King Tutankhamen ruled Egypt? As you read, try to answer this question.

King Tutankhamen

More than 3,300 years ago, Tutankhamen became pharaoh, or king, of Egypt. Before Tutankhamen became king, two of his relatives ruled. While these relatives were rulers, the people of Egypt were in religious **conflict.** One of the relatives made a terrible mistake. He did not allow people to worship any gods except Aten, the sun god. The Egyptians were furious. Egypt's priests fiercely opposed, or disagreed with, the king's one-god religion. They encouraged people to revolt, or rise up, against the king.

When the ruling king died, 9-year-old Tutankhamen became pharaoh. As king he had little power. In fact, he faced serious danger. Nearly all of his relatives had died. High-level advisors, or helpers, took care of him, but they also controlled him like a puppet. The nation was in **turmoil.** After Tutankhamen became pharaoh, the people of Egypt brought back the traditional religion. Egyptians again worshipped many gods. Most experts think that the boy king did not cause this **revival.** He may even have **retained** his belief in only Aten. This may have led to his downfall.

LANGUAGE CONNECTION

A simile compares two different objects or ideas using the words *like* or *as*. The phrase *controlled him like a puppet* is a simile. A puppet is a toy figure with arms and legs that a person can control by hand or with strings. What does it mean to *control someone like a puppet?*

People do not know very much about Tutankhamen's reign, but they know that it was short. "King Tut" died when he was 17 or 18 years old. People buried him in an elaborate tomb in the Valley of the Kings.

For years **rumors** spread about the existence of King Tut's tomb. In 1925 **archaeologist** Howard Carter located it in the valley. He carefully dug into the ground and uncovered one of the richest tombs ever found. The king was enclosed within a nest of three coffins. The king's body was mummified, or dried out and wrapped tightly with cloth for protection. The outer coffin was made of red quartzite stone. The middle coffin was made of wood covered with gold. The inner coffin, which held the mummy, was made of solid gold. The mummy itself was in poor condition. However, a magnificent gold mask covered the mummy's head.

Today people use the phrase *King Tut* to refer to a person of great wealth. Indeed, the tomb of the pharaoh held priceless objects of wonderful beauty. These objects included gold bracelets, anklets, collars, and necklace charms. The tomb also contained chairs, boxes, and chests that were carved from wood and covered with gold. These riches are among the most famous **artifacts** in the world.

CONTENT CONNECTION

What other artifacts have you seen in a museum or read about? What parts of the world are they from?

Ever since archaeologists opened the tomb, people have wondered how the king died. For decades experts believed that he had died of the lung disease tuberculosis. In 1968, however, X-rays of the mummy showed that the skull was broken. A severe blow, or hit, to the head had killed the pharaoh. Most historians, or people who study history, now believe that King Tut was murdered, or killed, by an advisor who was next in line to be king.

After You Read

A. Organizing Ideas

What do you know about King Tutankhamen? Complete the organizer below. Read the questions in the circles. Record your answers in the squares. Next to each answer, draw a picture or symbol that relates to the answer. Refer to the article for information. One answer has been done for you.

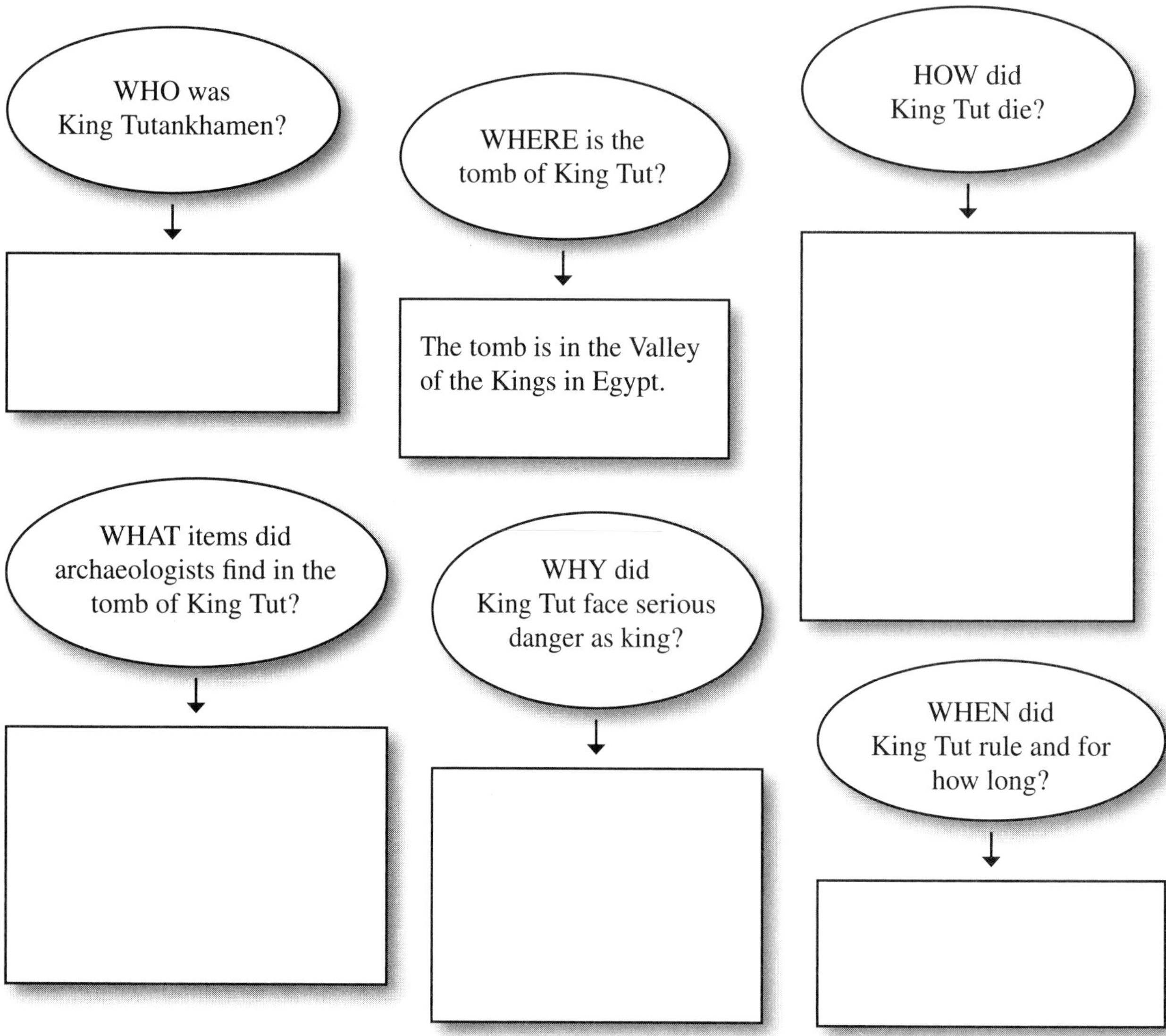

How did completing this organizer help you understand the article? What fact did you find most interesting about King Tut? Write two or more sentences to answer these questions. Would you use this type of organizer again? Why or why not?

B. Comprehension Skills

Tip! **Think about how to find answers.** Look back at what you read. The words in an answer are usually contained in a single sentence.

Mark box **a, b,** or **c** with an **X** before the choice that best completes each sentence.

Recalling Facts

1. King Tutankhamen ruled Egypt about
- ☐ **a.** 1,000 years ago.
- ☐ **b.** 2,500 years ago.
- ☐ **c.** 3,300 years ago.

2. One of the kings before Tutankhamen made people furious when he
- ☐ **a.** became too rich and powerful.
- ☐ **b.** encouraged people to revolt against the priests.
- ☐ **c.** did not allow them to worship any gods except Aten.

3. Tutankhamen became pharaoh when he was
- ☐ **a.** 9 years old.
- ☐ **b.** 18 years old.
- ☐ **c.** 33 years old.

4. Tutankhamen was controlled by
- ☐ **a.** the priests.
- ☐ **b.** his advisors.
- ☐ **c.** his closest friends.

5. In 1968 X-rays showed that King Tutankhamen had
- ☐ **a.** died of tuberculosis.
- ☐ **b.** broken his arm as a child.
- ☐ **c.** been killed by a blow to the head.

Understanding Ideas

1. The two kings who ruled before Tutankhamen both
- ☐ **a.** faced religious conflict.
- ☐ **b.** believed in one god.
- ☐ **c.** had many advisors.

2. Tutankhamen faced danger because
- ☐ **a.** he was very ill and weak.
- ☐ **b.** the kingdom was losing money.
- ☐ **c.** the kingdom was unstable after years of conflict.

3. One sign that the Egyptians respected their pharaohs is that Tutankhamen
- ☐ **a.** received help from advisors.
- ☐ **b.** was buried in an elaborate tomb.
- ☐ **c.** started a religious revival.

4. From the article, you can conclude that
- ☐ **a.** Egyptians greatly valued gold.
- ☐ **b.** tuberculosis was common in ancient Egypt.
- ☐ **c.** Egyptian artists had few materials to work with.

5. The article suggests that the objects in the tomb of King Tut
- ☐ **a.** are beautiful but overvalued.
- ☐ **b.** deserve the high value that people place on them.
- ☐ **c.** do not look as beautiful as they did thousands of years ago.

C. Reading Strategies

1. Recognizing Words in Context

Find the word *furious* in the article. One definition below is closest to the meaning of that word. One definition has the opposite or nearly the opposite meaning. The remaining definition has a meaning that has nothing to do with the word. Label the definitions **C** for *closest,* **O** for *opposite* or *nearly opposite,* and **U** for *unrelated.*

_____ **a.** pleased
_____ **b.** angry
_____ **c.** curious

2. Distinguishing Fact from Opinion

Two of the statements below present *facts,* which can be proved. The other statement is an *opinion,* which expresses someone's thoughts or beliefs. Label the statements **F** for *fact* and **O** for *opinion.*

_____ **a.** King Tut was too young to be pharaoh.
_____ **b.** King Tut died from a heavy blow to his head.
_____ **c.** King Tut's body was mummified after he died.

3. Making Correct Inferences

Two of the statements below are correct *inferences,* or reasonable guesses, that are based on information in the article. The other statement is an incorrect, or faulty, inference. Label the statements **C** for *correct* inference and **I** for *incorrect* inference.

_____ **a.** King Tut was not allowed to make decisions on his own.
_____ **b.** King Tut's advisors may have been more interested in power than in helping the king.
_____ **c.** King Tut probably did not believe in Aten, the sun god.

4. Understanding Main Ideas

One of the statements below expresses the main idea of the article. Another statement is too general, or too broad. The other explains only part of the article; it is too narrow. Label the statements **M** for *main idea,* **B** for *too broad,* and **N** for *too narrow.*

_____ **a.** The tomb of King Tutankhamen is in the Valley of the Kings.
_____ **b.** Kings called pharaohs once ruled ancient Egypt.
_____ **c.** King Tut was a young pharaoh whose tomb contained many riches.

5. Responding to the Article

Complete the following sentence in your own words:
From reading "King Tutankhamen," I have learned

____

____

D. Expanding Vocabulary

Content-Area Words

Cross out one word or phrase in each row that is not related to the word in dark type.

1. turmoil	confusion	unrest	feeling	thickness
2. revival	renew	bring back	burial	again
3. rumors	tombs	stories	talk	may be untrue
4. archaeologist	dig	remains	designer	ancient
5. artifacts	tools	ancient	priests	objects

Academic English

In the article "King Tutankhamen," you learned that *conflict* is a noun that means "disagreement." *Conflict* (kən flikt′) can also be a verb that means "to directly disagree with" or "to get in the way of," as in the following sentence.

Tom's story about the broken window seems to conflict with Jin's story.

Complete the sentence below.

1. JoJo's actions *conflict* with the rule that ______________________________

Now use the word *conflict* in a sentence of your own.

2. ______________________________

____

You also learned that *retained* means "continued to have or hold." *Retained* can also mean "held back" or "contained," as in the following sentence.

The new jar retained water, but the cracked jar did not.

Complete the sentence below.

3. The dam *retained* the river water from the lake until the dam ______________________________

Now use the word *retained* in two sentences of your own.

4. ______________________________

5. ______________________________

Share your new sentences with a partner.

Lesson 7

The History of Soccer

Before You Read

Think about what you know. Read the lesson title above. Think about what you already know about soccer. Have you ever played or watched others play soccer? What is your favorite sport to play?

Vocabulary

The content-area and academic English words below appear in "The History of Soccer." Read the definitions and the example sentences.

Content-Area Words

defeated (di fēt′əd) having lost a competition or battle; beaten
Example: The *defeated* team did not get to go to the play-offs.

vulgar (vul′gər) in poor taste; with bad manners
Example: Many think boxing is *vulgar* because the athletes hit each other.

association (ə sō′sē ā′shən) an organized group of people with common interests or purposes
Example: The American Heart *Association* educates people about how to keep their hearts healthy.

propel (prə pel′) to cause something to move forward
Example: The wheels of a bike turn and *propel* the bike into motion.

penalty (pen′əl tē) a punishment for breaking a law or a rule
Example: The *penalty* for anyone who cheats on a test is a failing grade.

Academic English

contact (kon′takt) the act of two things touching
Example: The *contact* between Iri's sweater and her skin made her feel itchy.

automatic (ô′tə mat′ik) done without extra thought or outside control
Example: When my dog sees me, his *automatic* response is to wag his tail.

Rate each vocabulary word according to the following scale. Write a number next to each content-area and academic English word.

4 I have never seen the word before.
3 I have seen the word but do not know what it means.
2 I know what the word means when I read it.
1 I use the word myself in speaking or writing.

Now skim the article and look for other words that are new to you. Write each new word and its definition in the Personal Dictionary.

While You Read

Think about why you read. People around the world like to play soccer. How did this sport begin, and how did it become so popular? As you read, look for the main idea about the history of soccer.

The History of Soccer

Japanese records from 1004 B.C. describe a game in which players kicked a ball around a field. This game may have been an early form of soccer. However, some sports historians believe that the game of soccer began in England in the third century. They claim that early English warriors, or soldiers, kicked around the head of a **defeated** enemy. Whether or not this is true, soccer certainly is an ancient sport.

There is no doubt that the English played soccer during the reign, or rule, of King Edward I in the 1300s. In fact, the king passed a law against soccer. The law stated, "There is great noise . . . caused by hustling over large balls from which many evils may arise." People who were caught as they played soccer were sent to prison. Two hundred years later, during the reign of Queen Elizabeth I, people still were sent to jail if they played this "**vulgar**" sport.

LANGUAGE CONNECTION

A homophone is a word that sounds the same as another word but has a different meaning. Look at the word *reign*. It sounds like the word *rain*. What does each word mean?

Even with these laws, soccer grew more and more popular. In 1681 it became an official sport in England. By the 1800s, people throughout the country played soccer. By the 1900s, even boys from rich families played it at private schools. Today soccer is popular with most English people.

In 1843 officials met at an English school to suggest the first rules for the sport. In 1863 the heads of English soccer teams met in London to agree on some official rules. They organized an English soccer **association.** By 1871 all of the English soccer clubs were following these rules. Today all soccer teams play by them.

People in most countries know soccer as *football*. Only the United States uses the term *soccer*. The rules are simple. Eleven people play on each side. They play the game on a field, called a *pitch*, which is 75 yards wide and 120 yards long. A net called a *goal* stands at each end of the pitch. The net is 8 yards wide and 8 feet high. The object of the game is to get the ball into the other team's goal. A goalie blocks the goal to try to prevent the ball from going into it. Goalies may catch the ball with their hands. They are the only players who can have this kind of **contact** with the ball. No other players may touch the ball with their hands. Players may **propel** the ball with their legs and feet or with their heads. They may control the ball with any part of the body except their hands. A *hand ball* receives an **automatic penalty.**

CONTENT CONNECTION

When a soccer player kicks the ball into the net, he or she scores a goal. Can you think of any other sports in which players score points when they get a ball or other object into a net?

Soccer is by far the most popular sport in the world. Every four years, nearly every nation in the world competes in the World Cup soccer tournament. Billions of soccer fans from around the world watch the World Cup on television.

After You Read

A. Organizing Ideas

What events helped make soccer into the sport it is today? Complete the time line below. On the lines, write down the dates of important events in the history of soccer. In the box below each date, explain what happened at that time. Some have been done for you.

Time Line of Soccer

third century

____

____

King Edward I passed a law against soccer.

1681

____

____

Officials met at an English school to suggest rules for the game.

____

____

Today

____

What information from the article did this time line help you remember? Write two or more sentences to answer this question. Then look back at the article. What information does not fit into a time line? How could you organize that information?

____

____

____

B. Comprehension Skills

 **Think about how to find answers.** Look back at different parts of the text. What facts help you figure out how to complete the sentences?

Mark box **a, b,** or **c** with an **X** before the choice that best completes each sentence.

Recalling Facts

1. Some people think that soccer started when English warriors

☐ **a.** traveled to Japan.
☐ **b.** learned it in prison.
☐ **c.** kicked around the head of an enemy.

2. Before the mid-1800s, soccer was played differently in different places because

☐ **a.** it was still illegal to play soccer.
☐ **b.** the game had no official rules yet.
☐ **c.** England had very few soccer teams.

3. A soccer team scores a point when

☐ **a.** the goalie catches the ball.
☐ **b.** the ball enters the other team's net.
☐ **c.** a player on the other team touches the ball with his or her hands.

4. A soccer player gets a penalty when he or she

☐ **a.** kicks the ball out of the pitch.
☐ **b.** touches the ball with his or her hands.
☐ **c.** hits the ball into the goal with his or her head.

5. The World Cup is played by

☐ **a.** college teams.
☐ **b.** only English teams.
☐ **c.** teams from many countries.

Understanding Ideas

1. From the article, you can conclude that

☐ **a.** Queen Elizabeth I liked soccer.
☐ **b.** soccer is more than 500 years old.
☐ **c.** children in private schools no longer like to play soccer.

2. You can also conclude that, over the years,

☐ **a.** nothing could keep people away from soccer.
☐ **b.** soccer has been enjoyed mostly by rich families.
☐ **c.** many people in the world have lost interest in soccer.

3. The main idea of the article is that

☐ **a.** soccer began in England.
☐ **b.** the English played soccer during the reign of King Edward I.
☐ **c.** soccer has become popular throughout the world.

4. People decided to write official rules for soccer probably because

☐ **a.** some teams cheated.
☐ **b.** the game was too noisy and violent without rules.
☐ **c.** teams had disagreements about how to play the game.

5. The author of the article would probably agree that

☐ **a.** soccer is a popular game.
☐ **b.** the rules of soccer are unfair.
☐ **c.** American football should be more popular than soccer.

C. Reading Strategies

1. Recognizing Words in Context

Find the word *prevent* in the article. One definition below is closest to the meaning of that word. One definition has the opposite or nearly the opposite meaning. The remaining definition has a meaning that has nothing to do with the word. Label the definitions **C** for *closest,* **O** for *opposite* or *nearly opposite,* and **U** for *unrelated.*

_____ **a.** stop

_____ **b.** break

_____ **c.** allow

2. Distinguishing Fact from Opinion

Two of the statements below present *facts,* which can be proved. The other statement is an *opinion,* which expresses someone's thoughts or beliefs. Label the statements **F** for *fact* and **O** for *opinion.*

_____ **a.** Goalies are the only soccer players who are allowed to touch the ball with their hands.

_____ **b.** Soccer was popular even when it was illegal.

_____ **c.** Americans should call soccer *football* as the rest of the world does.

3. Making Correct Inferences

Two of the statements below are correct *inferences,* or reasonable guesses, that are based on information in the article. The other statement is an incorrect, or faulty, inference. Label the statements **C** for *correct* inference and **I** for *incorrect* inference.

_____ **a.** Soccer players who are not the goalie may try to keep the ball out of the net with any part of their bodies except their hands.

_____ **b.** People need to be tall to play soccer.

_____ **c.** No one is completely sure how the game of soccer began.

4. Understanding Main Ideas

One of the statements below expresses the main idea of the article. Another statement is too general, or too broad. The other explains only part of the article; it is too narrow. Label the statements **M** for *main idea,* **B** for *too broad,* and **N** for *too narrow.*

_____ **a.** Soccer is the most popular sport in the world.

_____ **b.** People have enjoyed soccer since before it had rules, and it is still popular today.

_____ **c.** The object of soccer is to get the ball into the other team's goal.

5. Responding to the Article

Complete the following sentence in your own words:

One thing in "The History of Soccer" that I cannot understand is

____

____

D. Expanding Vocabulary

Content-Area Words

Complete each sentence with a word from the box. Write the missing word on the line.

defeated	vulgar	association	propel	penalty

1. Students may get in trouble if they use ________________ words.
2. The tennis player who won shook hands with the ________________ player.
3. People who leave trash in the park have to pay a ________________ of $25.
4. The ________________ of horse owners sends its members a newsletter each month.
5. Dolphins use their tails to ________________ themselves through the water.

Academic English

In the article "The History of Soccer," you learned that *contact* means "the act of two things touching." *Contact* can also mean "the state of being in communication with someone," as in the following sentence.

Tran said that she would be in contact with me by phone.

Complete the sentence below.

1. I lost *contact* with my friends when ________________________________

Now use the word *contact* in a sentence of your own.

2. ____

____

You also learned that *automatic* means "done without extra thought or outside control." *Automatic* can also mean "having machine parts that operate or control themselves," as in the following sentence.

The automatic coffeemaker starts to make coffee every morning at 6:00 A.M.

Complete the sentence below.

3. I know that the garage door is *automatic* because ________________________________

Now use the word *automatic* in two sentences of your own.

4. ____
5. ____

Share your new sentences with a partner.

Space Technology and Geography

Before You Read

Think about what you know. Read the title and the first paragraph of the article on the opposite page. What does the word *space* make you think about? How do you think it relates to geography?

Vocabulary

The content-area and academic English words below appear in "Space Technology and Geography." Read the definitions and the example sentences.

Content-Area Words

launched (lôncht) pushed or put into motion—especially into the air

Example: The wind *launched* the kite into the sky.

satellite (sat′əl īt′) an object that travels around a body in space, such as Earth

Example: A *satellite* in space may take pictures of Earth.

missions (mish′ənz) specific tasks that groups of people accomplish

Example: Mountain rescue teams have search *missions* to find lost people.

astronauts (as′trə nôts′) people who fly or operate a spacecraft

Example: The first spacecraft to land on the Moon carried three *astronauts*.

erosion (i rō′zhən) the process in which wind or water slowly wears down or washes away soil and rock

Example: *Erosion* from ocean waves has worn away the rock on the beach.

Academic English

technology (tek nol′ə jē) methods and devices that help expand scientific knowledge in a certain field of study

Example: Special *technology* helps scientists study Earth from space.

precise (pri sīs′) very exact

Example: These *precise* directions helped me find the house easily.

Read again the example sentences that follow the content-area and academic English word definitions. With a partner, discuss the meanings of the words and sentences. Then make up a sentence of your own for each word. Your teacher may wish to discuss your new sentences in class.

Now skim the article and look for other words that are new to you. Write each new word and its definition in the Personal Dictionary.

While You Read

Think about why you read. What would it be like to take pictures of Earth from space? What features on Earth's surface would the pictures show? As you read, try to find the answer.

Space Technology and Geography

Geography is the study of features on the surface of Earth. Scientists use geography to study global warming and to track the weather. Governments use it to learn where people live and work. They also use it to plan what to do with the land. Today a science called space **technology** makes it easier than ever to use geography.

The United States **launched** its first **satellite** in 1958. Many space **missions** followed. Some of the missions involved geographical studies. In fact, Earth science is a big part of the work of the National Air and Space Administration (NASA).

Astronauts in the first space shuttle decided to take photographs of Earth from their position in space. Over the years, the quality of the pictures has improved. Shuttle photography now shows land features, such as rivers. Photographs may even show the streets of large cities. Photos of the same places at different times show ways that the land is changing.

NASA does not use only photographs. In 1958 it launched TIROS (the Television Infrared Observation Satellite). This satellite was the first satellite to study Earth. It gives effective weather forecasts. It also has led scientists to create new space tools that help study geography.

The Landsat Program began in 1972. This satellite sends detailed views of Earth from space. The pictures are so **precise** that scientists can count the number of crops in a field. Landsat shows where Earth's surface has faults, or cracks. These faults are places where earthquakes may occur. This information helps people plan new cities and factories. Landsat has also made discoveries. It located ranges of unknown mountains in Antarctica. It pinpointed small lakes in Virginia that were not on maps. Landsat is now even more advanced, and it still flies today.

The Earth Observing-1 (EO-1) is another space tool. This spacecraft flies right behind Landsat. It takes pictures of the same places. When people look at the two sets of pictures together, they can see how cities grow. They can also see how other places, such as rain forests, shrink over time. This helps scientists learn how people affect geography.

The Geographical Information Systems (GIS) is one of the newest space tools. GIS is computer software. It obtains, or gets, data from satellites. This data helps scientists study Earth. GIS has allowed scientists to note changes to Earth's surface, such as **erosion** on the coast of Israel. GIS is different from earlier space tools. People outside governments can use it. Businesses, schools, and even regular people can use GIS to see how changes to the planet may affect them.

CONTENT CONNECTION

The largest satellite that currently orbits Earth is the International Space Station. More than 90 percent of the world's population will be able to see this space station when it is finished. What do you think the space station will look like from Earth?

LANGUAGE CONNECTION

The word *pinpointed* means "found the exact place of something." What two words make up the word *pinpointed?* What do they mean?

After You Read

A. Organizing Ideas

What kinds of space technology are useful to people who study geography? Complete the chart below. In each circle, write down the name of one kind of space technology. Then write down at least two facts about each kind. Refer to the article for information. Some have been done for you.

Kinds of Space Technology

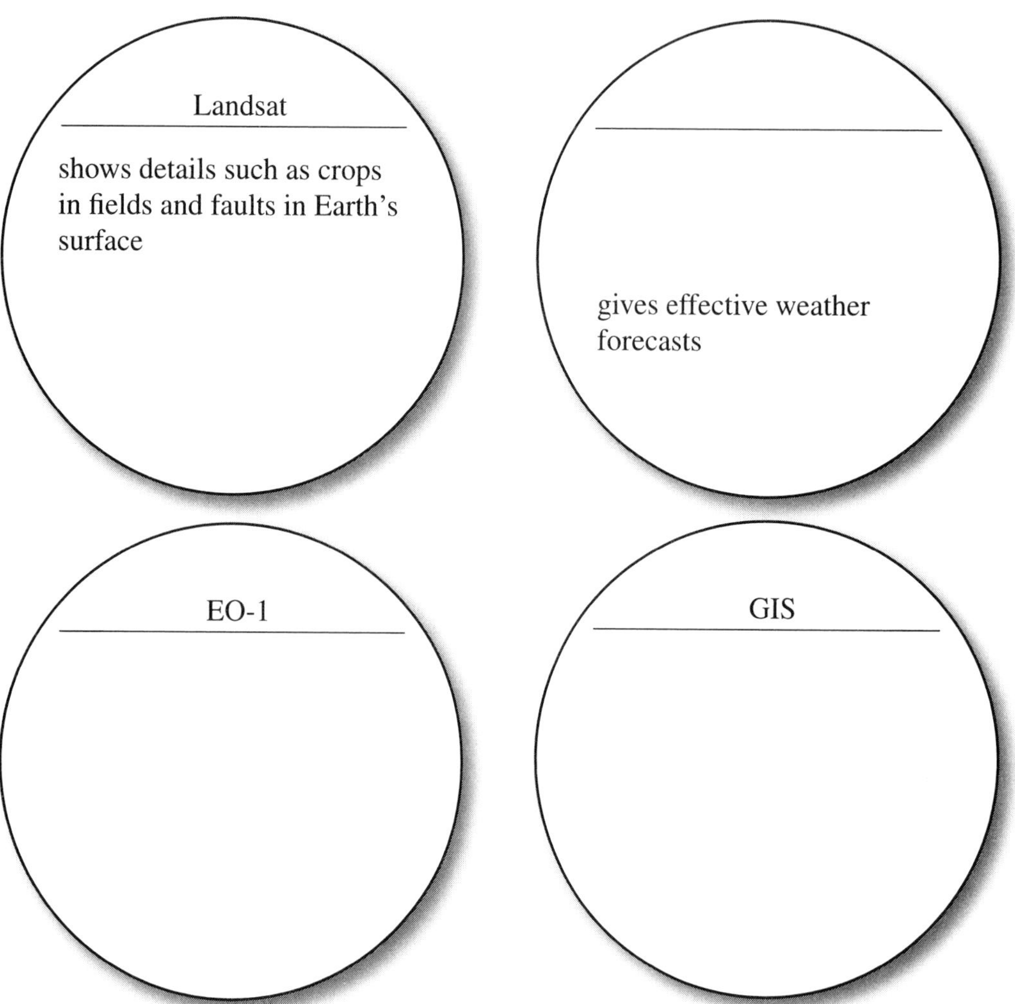

Did this chart help you understand how space technology and geography are related? Which technology do you think is most helpful for the study of Earth? Write two or more sentences to answer these questions. Was this chart a useful way to organize information? Why or why not?

____

____

____

B. Comprehension Skills

Think about how to find answers. Think about what each sentence means. Try to say it to yourself in your own words before you complete it.

Mark box **a, b,** or **c** with an **X** before the choice that best completes each sentence.

Recalling Facts

1. The United States launched its first satellite in

☐ **a.** 1958.
☐ **b.** 1972.
☐ **c.** 1999.

2. Governments study geography in order to

☐ **a.** set laws.
☐ **b.** improve business plans.
☐ **c.** plan what to do with land.

3. Scientists use TIROS to

☐ **a.** predict the weather.
☐ **b.** take photos of Earth.
☐ **c.** launch other satellites.

4. Landsat was able to

☐ **a.** track weather systems.
☐ **b.** take pictures of other planets.
☐ **c.** discover mountains in Antarctica.

5. GIS is a special space tool because it

☐ **a.** is the largest satellite.
☐ **b.** can be used by regular people.
☐ **c.** was the first satellite to orbit Earth.

Understanding Ideas

1. From the article, you can conclude that recent U.S. satellites are

☐ **a.** similar to older ones.
☐ **b.** limited in their usefulness.
☐ **c.** more advanced than older ones.

2. Space tools help businesses decide where not to build because they show

☐ **a.** the growth pattern of cities.
☐ **b.** how rain forests are shrinking.
☐ **c.** where earthquakes may occur.

3. EO-1 takes photographs of the same places as Landsat

☐ **a.** because Landsat is old and cannot take clear pictures.
☐ **b.** so that scientists can compare the two sets of pictures.
☐ **c.** because EO-1 is practicing for future photography missions.

4. The fact that Landsat has discovered new mountains and lakes probably means that

☐ **a.** the satellite made an error.
☐ **b.** those features have developed on Earth's surface only recently.
☐ **c.** satellite images show more detail than older mapmaking methods.

5. The main idea of the article is that

☐ **a.** space technology helps scientists learn more about Earth.
☐ **b.** GIS makes it possible for everyone to use space technology.
☐ **c.** space technology has made many advances since 1958.

C. Reading Strategies

1. Recognizing Words in Context

Find the word *shrink* in the article. One definition below is closest to the meaning of that word. One definition has the opposite or nearly the opposite meaning. The remaining definition has a meaning that has nothing to do with the word. Label the definitions **C** for *closest,* **O** for *opposite* or *nearly opposite,* and **U** for *unrelated.*

_____ **a.** look bigger

_____ **b.** become smaller

_____ **c.** grow larger

2. Distinguishing Fact from Opinion

Two of the statements below present *facts,* which can be proved. The other statement is an *opinion,* which expresses someone's thoughts or beliefs. Label the statements **F** for *fact* and **O** for *opinion.*

_____ **a.** Satellites cost too much money to operate.

_____ **b.** Scientists can use satellites to figure out where earthquakes may occur.

_____ **c.** Some satellites help people study the weather on Earth.

3. Making Correct Inferences

Two of the statements below are correct *inferences,* or reasonable guesses, that are based on information in the article. The other statement is an incorrect, or faulty, inference. Label the statements **C** for *correct* inference and **I** for *incorrect* inference.

_____ **a.** People need a computer in order to use GIS.

_____ **b.** City planners do not want to place buildings along faults.

_____ **c.** The United States launched the first satellite in history.

4. Understanding Main Ideas

One of the statements below expresses the main idea of the article. Another statement is too general, or too broad. The other explains only part of the article; it is too narrow. Label the statements **M** for *main idea,* **B** for *too broad,* and **N** for *too narrow.*

_____ **a.** Different tools help scientists study Earth from space.

_____ **b.** Space technology and geography are related.

_____ **c.** GIS obtains data from satellites.

5. Responding to the Article

Complete the following sentence in your own words:

Before reading "Space Technology and Geography," I already knew

____

____

D. Expanding Vocabulary

Content-Area Words

Read each item carefully. Write on the line the word or phrase that best completes each sentence.

1. The boys launched the ______________________ from the middle of a field.
   rocket grass school
2. A ______________________ may cause erosion.
   bird river rose
3. A satellite travels ______________________ an object in space.
   around under behind
4. The main job of astronauts is to ______________________.
   study geography write speeches complete space missions
5. People who do mountain rescue missions must ______________________ the mountains.
   enjoy be familiar with take pictures of

Academic English

In the article "Space Technology and Geography," you learned that *technology* means "methods and devices that help expand scientific knowledge in a certain field of study." In the article, *technology* refers to methods and devices used to study Earth from space. *Technology* can also refer to methods and devices used to do other things, as in the following sentence.

New technology helps factories build cars more quickly.

Complete the sentence below.

1. Computer *technology* helps people around the world to ______________________

Now use the word *technology* in a sentence of your own.

2. ______________________

You also learned that *precise* means "very exact." *Precise* can also mean "being exactly the right amount," as in the following sentence.

Flora added the precise amount of sugar that the cookie recipe called for.

Complete the sentence below.

3. Carlos mixed a *precise* amount of red paint with ______________________

Now use the word *precise* in two sentences of your own.

4. ______________________
5. ______________________

Share your new sentences with a partner.

Creoles and Cajuns in Louisiana

Before You Read

Think about what you know. Read the title and the first sentence of the article on the opposite page. Have you ever heard of Creoles or Cajuns? What words describe groups of people you know about?

Vocabulary

The content-area and academic English words below appear in "Creoles and Cajuns in Louisiana." Read the definitions and the example sentences.

Content-Area Words

colonies (kol′ə nēz) lands that are under the control of another country
Example: Britain ruled 13 *colonies* in America before the Revolutionary War.

classes (klas′əz) groups of people who have the same importance in society
Example: In some countries, the upper *classes* have more rights than the lower classes do.

lured (loord) created a powerful interest; attracted
Example: The delicious smell of the food *lured* me into the kitchen.

elite (i lēt′) best; most select
Example: The *elite* school only accepts students with very high grades.

confusion (kən fū′zhən) the state of having disordered or mixed ideas or thoughts
Example: The students felt *confusion* about the new topic in math class.

Academic English

undergo (un′dər gō′) to pass through
Example: The girls will *undergo* lessons to learn how to play tennis.

incorporate (in kôr′pə rāt′) to include as a part
Example: The musical play will *incorporate* several songs from one band.

Complete the sentences below that contain the content-area and academic English words above. Use the spaces provided. The first one has been done for you.

1. A person may feel *confusion* if he or she gets lost.
2. Countries probably would not let their *colonies* ________.
3. I like meals that *incorporate* both ________.
4. The pond will *undergo* change in the winter when ________.
5. The store put up signs that *lured* ________.
6. People in different social *classes* probably ________.
7. An *elite* restaurant probably serves ________.

Now skim the article and look for other words that are new to you. Write each new word and its definition in the Personal Dictionary.

While You Read

Tip! **Think about why you read.** Throughout history people have come to America from many parts of the world. Where did Creoles and Cajuns come from, and what did they bring with them? As you read, try to answer these questions.

Creoles and Cajuns in Louisiana

Creoles and Cajuns are two groups of people who live in Louisiana. Both groups settled there long ago and have ancestors who came from France. Both groups have interesting histories, as do the words *Creole* and *Cajun.*

The English word *Creole* comes from the French, Spanish, and Portuguese languages. In France, Spain, and Portugal, *Creole* referred to a European citizen who was born in the **colonies** in America. However, in Louisiana, *Creole* referred to a person born in that state. Creole families were the first to settle in the region. Most of the early Creole settlers belonged to the French upper **classes.** Some of these settlers wanted to be part of the upper class in their new land. Since the Civil War, American society has changed. Today the largest Creole community lives in southeastern Louisiana. Many live in New Orleans.

The word *Cajun* comes from the word *Acadian.* This group also came from France. They settled in eastern Canada. They named the settlement Acadia. The Acadians had been poor peasants in France. In their new home, they became farmers. In 1755 some Acadians left their settlement after the British defeated the French in Canada. The French culture in Louisiana **lured** some Acadians to move there. Most Cajuns today live in the southwestern part of Louisiana. At first the Cajuns did not get along well with the Creoles. However, some of the Cajuns eventually married into the **elite** Creole society.

Words can **undergo** change over time. The term *Creole* has had many meanings. This can cause **confusion.** In the past, some people called themselves Creoles to show that they were not Cajuns. Today the word has a broader, or less specific, meaning. People often use the word *Creole* to describe Cajun things. It may also describe purely Creole things.

Both cultures **incorporate** many influences. For example, the Cajun French language includes African and English words. Creole music, called Zydeco, combines French folk music with African rhythms. The words of the songs are often in Creole French. Creole food recipes often include peppers from Mexico. They also include herbs that grow wild in Louisiana. Gumbo, a thick soup, contains tomatoes, onions, and a vegetable called *okra.* It also contains chicken and sausage. Many people think that the name of the soup comes from the African word *gambo,* which means "okra."

LANGUAGE CONNECTION

The verb *settled* means "began to live in a place." As you read, you will see the words *settlers* and *settlement.* What do these words mean? What parts of speech are they?

CONTENT CONNECTION

Mardi Gras is a French holiday that people now celebrate in New Orleans. Early Creoles celebrated Mardi Gras on the banks of the Mississippi River. During the celebration, people have parades and parties. What festivals does your culture celebrate?

After You Read

A. Organizing Ideas

How are Creoles and Cajuns similar and different? Complete the diagram below. In the left circle, list facts about Creoles. In the right circle, list facts about Cajuns. In the section where the two circles overlap, list facts that apply to both Creoles and Cajuns. Use the article to help you. Some have been done for you.

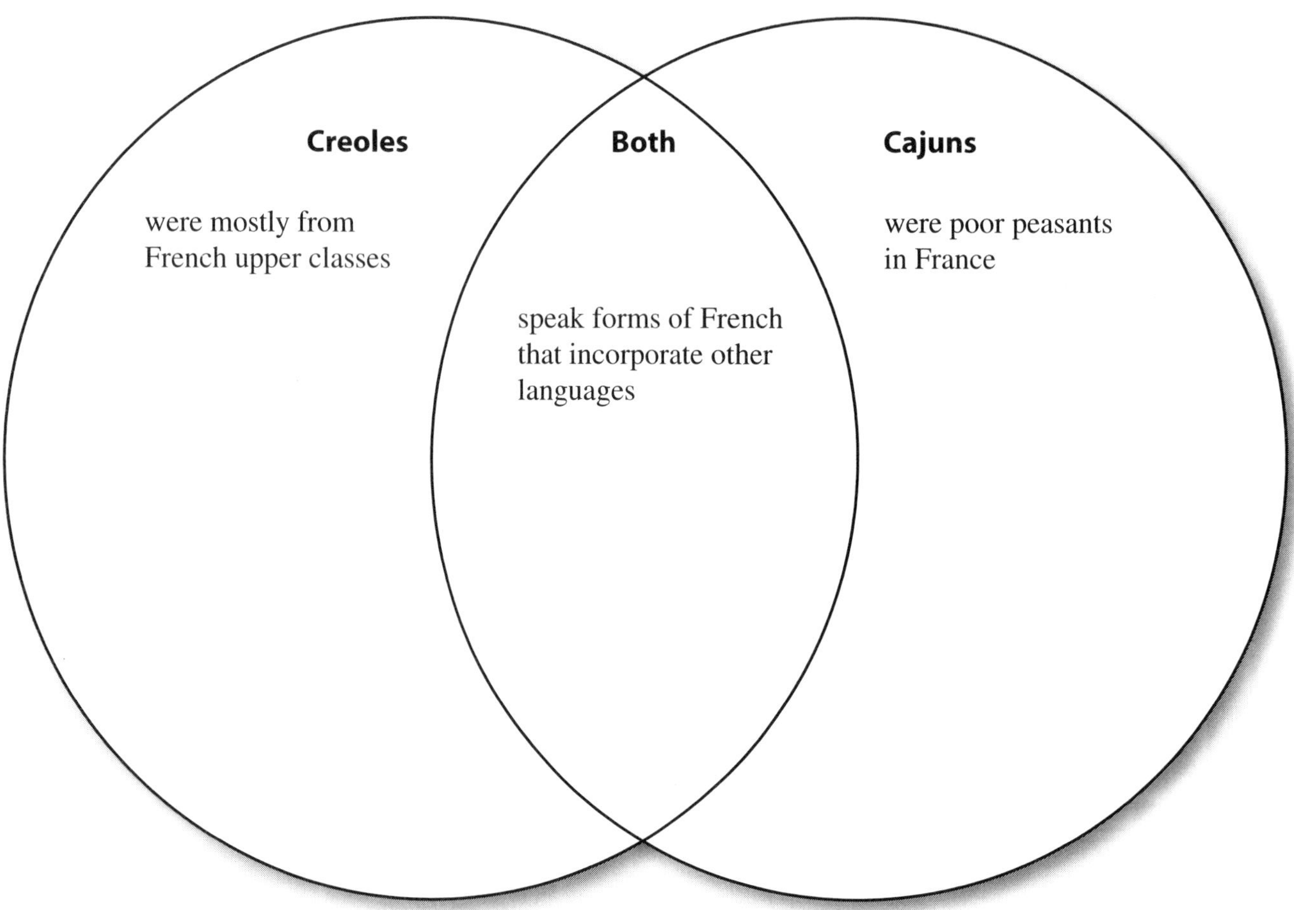

How did the diagram help you understand the similarities and differences between Creoles and Cajuns? Write two or more sentences to answer this question. When could you use this type of diagram again?

B. Comprehension Skills

Tip! **Think about how to find answers.** Look back at what you read. The information is in the text, but you may have to look in several sentences to find it.

Mark box **a, b,** or **c** with an **X** before the choice that best completes each sentence.

Recalling Facts

1. Creoles and Cajuns are people who
- ☐ **a.** continue to speak Spanish.
- ☐ **b.** came from France and settled in Louisiana.
- ☐ **c.** came from Mexico and settled in Louisiana.

2. The English word *Creole*
- ☐ **a.** comes from three other languages.
- ☐ **b.** was created by Americans.
- ☐ **c.** describes people who have just moved to Louisiana.

3. The word *Cajun*
- ☐ **a.** is Portuguese.
- ☐ **b.** means "peasant."
- ☐ **c.** comes from the word *Acadian*.

4. Creole life in Louisiana is
- ☐ **a.** a mixture of many influences.
- ☐ **b.** famous for its very plain food.
- ☐ **c.** very different from life in other places in the United States.

5. Gumbo is a
- ☐ **a.** thick soup.
- ☐ **b.** kind of French folk music.
- ☐ **c.** name for part of Louisiana.

Understanding Ideas

1. From the article, you can conclude that the meaning of a word
- ☐ **a.** never changes.
- ☐ **b.** may change over time.
- ☐ **c.** is always clear at any given time.

2. You can also conclude that immigrants from the same place
- ☐ **a.** rarely settle together.
- ☐ **b.** always share the same values.
- ☐ **c.** may bring different experiences and values to their new home.

3. The mixture of influences in the Creole and Cajun cultures shows that people
- ☐ **a.** often ignore other cultures.
- ☐ **b.** follow only their own traditions.
- ☐ **c.** may use ideas from other cultures.

4. A person who wants to experience Creole culture should visit
- ☐ **a.** Canada.
- ☐ **b.** southern Louisiana.
- ☐ **c.** any city in the South.

5. The main idea of the article is that
- ☐ **a.** the United States is a mixture of many influences.
- ☐ **b.** Creoles and Cajuns have shaped a new culture in the United States.
- ☐ **c.** the words *Creole* and *Cajun* have had different meanings over time.

C. Reading Strategies

1. Recognizing Words in Context

Find the word *ancestors* in the article. One definition below is closest to the meaning of that word. One definition has the opposite or nearly the opposite meaning. The remaining definition has a meaning that has nothing to do with the word. Label the definitions **C** for *closest,* **O** for *opposite* or *nearly opposite,* and **U** for *unrelated.*

____ **a.** family members who lived long ago
____ **b.** family members who have just been born
____ **c.** close friends of the family

2. Distinguishing Fact from Opinion

Two of the statements below present *facts,* which can be proved. The other statement is an *opinion,* which expresses someone's thoughts or beliefs. Label the statements **F** for *fact* and **O** for *opinion.*

____ **a.** At one time, Creoles and Cajuns did not get along.
____ **b.** It is better to be a Creole in Louisiana than a Cajun.
____ **c.** Some Acadians left Canada to live in Louisiana.

3. Making Correct Inferences

Two of the statements below are correct *inferences,* or reasonable guesses, that are based on information in the article. The other statement is an incorrect, or faulty, inference. Label the statements **C** for *correct* inference and **I** for *incorrect* inference.

____ **a.** The Creoles and Cajuns belonged to different classes in France.
____ **b.** Most people can tell the Creole and Cajun cultures apart easily.
____ **c.** African culture has influenced both the Creole and Cajun cultures.

4. Understanding Main Ideas

One of the statements below expresses the main idea of the article. Another statement is too general, or too broad. The other explains only part of the article; it is too narrow. Label the statements **M** for *main idea,* **B** for *too broad,* and **N** for *too narrow.*

____ **a.** Creoles and Cajuns are two groups of people who live in Louisiana.
____ **b.** Creoles live in southeastern Louisiana, and Cajuns live in southwestern Louisiana.
____ **c.** Creoles and Cajuns came from France and formed a new culture in Louisiana.

5. Responding to the Article

Complete the following sentence in your own words:

One thing in "Creoles and Cajuns in Louisiana" that I cannot understand is

____

____

D. Expanding Vocabulary

Content-Area Words

Complete each sentence with a word from the box. Write the missing word on the line.

colonies	classes	lured	elite	confusion

1. Before the United States became a country, the states were ________________.
2. The cheese ________________ the mouse into the trap.
3. Diners pay a great deal of money for lunch at the ________________ restaurant.
4. The book caused ________________ about whether or not diets are a good idea.
5. People may enter different social ________________ through wealth or marriage.

Academic English

In the article "Creoles and Cajuns in Louisiana," you learned that *undergo* means "to pass through." *Undergo* can also mean "to suffer" or "to endure," as in the following sentence.

I had to undergo a painful visit to the dentist.

Complete the sentence below.

1. Fue had to *undergo* punishment because he ________________________________

Now use the word *undergo* in a sentence of your own.

2. ____

____

You also learned that *incorporate* means "to include as a part." *Incorporate* can also mean "to combine into a whole," as in the following sentence.

Joaquín will incorporate violets and lilies into a bouquet for his mother.

Complete the sentence below.

3. Nahee stirred the drink mix to *incorporate* ________________________________

Now use the word *incorporate* in two sentences of your own.

4. ____
5. ____

Share your new sentences with a partner.

Historical Fiction

Before You Read

Think about what you know. Read the title and the first two sentences of the article on the opposite page. What do you predict the article will be about? Have you ever read a book with a story that takes place in the past?

Vocabulary

The content-area and academic English words below appear in "Historical Fiction." Read the definitions and the example sentences.

Content-Area Words

historical (his tôr′i kəl) involving past events or people
Example: The first space flight was an important *historical* event.

novels (nov′əlz) long works of fiction that tell stories with characters
Example: My favorite books are mystery *novels.*

plot (plot) the main story of a book, movie, play, or poem
Example: The movie *plot* involved a family that got lost in the desert.

dialogue (dī′ə lôg′) conversation, or words spoken, between people in a story
Example: The jokes in the *dialogue* show that the characters are funny.

customs (kus′təmz) social traditions of a group of people
Example: Different cultures have different *customs* for how to greet someone.

Academic English

encounter (en koun′tər) to face or experience something difficult
Example: Jana will *encounter* many challenges as she trains to be a dancer.

contemporary (kən tem′pə rer′ē) current; modern
Example: *Contemporary* music often uses computers to make sounds.

Do any of the words above seem related? Sort the seven vocabulary words into two or more categories. Write the words down on note cards or in a chart. Words may fit into more than one group. You may wish to work with a partner for this activity.

Now skim the article and look for other words that are new to you. Write each new word and its definition in the Personal Dictionary.

While You Read

Think about why you read. What parts of a historical fiction story are true, and what parts does the author make up? As you read, try to answer this question.

Historical Fiction

Historical fiction is a key part of many social studies classes. Good historical fiction mixes facts with storytelling skill. These stories take place in the past. The main characters are almost always fictional, or made up by the author. These characters usually face a serious conflict. They **encounter** huge challenges. Often their lives are in danger. Two well-known historical fiction writers are Lois Lowry and Dolores Johnson.

Historical **novels** may help students get interested in history. The stories include historical facts. This means that students can learn about the past as they read. Dramatic tools, such as **plot, dialogue,** and conflict, help students enjoy the magic of a story. Students also connect with the characters they read about. This helps the students understand the time and place better.

Historical fiction uses true details to make the story seem real. Accuracy, or correctness, is very important in this form of writing. Authors carefully research the places and time periods for their books. As students read historical fiction, they can learn about clothing, food, and tools from a certain time in history. These details help students imagine the ways of life in other times. Students can also learn about speech patterns and social **customs** from historical novels. This knowledge helps them recognize how a culture has changed over time.

Historical fiction also helps connect the past to **contemporary** daily life. Students can view the characters almost as real people. This helps the students make important links between the past and their own lives.

Number the Stars, by Lois Lowry, is a good example of historical fiction. This story takes place during World War II. At that time, German soldiers called *Nazis* had taken over Denmark. The book tells how a 10-year-old girl and her family help another young girl to escape from Denmark. The book features made-up characters in a real setting, or time and place. The story contains true details about the war and about life during the 1940s.

Another good example of historical fiction is *Now Let Me Fly: The Story of a Slave Family,* by Dolores Johnson. It tells the story of Minna, a young African girl. A slave trader "buys" Minna and brings her to America. The author made up the character of Minna and set her story in the eighteenth century. The story gives the reader an accurate picture of what life was like for some enslaved African Americans of that time.

LANGUAGE CONNECTION

Some English words have more than one meaning. In the first sentence, the word *key* is an adjective that means "very important." What is another meaning for the word *key?* What part of speech is it?

CONTENT CONNECTION

Think of a historical period or event that you know about. How was life at that time different from life today? If you wrote a historical fiction book about that time, what characters would you make up? What story would you tell?

After You Read

A. Organizing Ideas

What do you know about historical fiction? Complete the outline below. On the lines, write sentences to answer the questions about historical fiction. Refer to the article for information. Some have been done for you.

Historical Fiction

I. What are some features of historical fiction?

A. Historical fiction stories take place in the past.

B. ____________________

C. ____________________

II. How does historical fiction help students get interested in history?

A. The story makes the past seem real.

B. ____________________

C. ____________________

III. What role do true details play in historical fiction?

A. ____________________

B. Details help students learn about clothing, food, and tools from the past.

C. ____________________

IV. What time periods would you like to read about in a historical fiction book?

A. ____________________

B. ____________________

C. ____________________

What have you learned from your outline? Write two or more sentences about one of the questions you answered. Did the outline help you organize the facts in a clear way? Explain your answer.

____

____

____

B. Comprehension Skills

Tip! **Think about how to find answers.** Read each sentence below. Underline the words that will help you figure out how to complete each item.

Mark box **a, b,** or **c** with an **X** before the choice that best completes each sentence.

Recalling Facts

1. Historical fiction mixes historical facts with
- ☐ **a.** art from the past.
- ☐ **b.** stories about made-up characters.
- ☐ **c.** information about people of today.

2. Historical novels are set in
- ☐ **a.** the past.
- ☐ **b.** the future.
- ☐ **c.** the present.

3. An important part of historical fiction is
- ☐ **a.** pictures.
- ☐ **b.** true details.
- ☐ **c.** complicated plots.

4. One dramatic tool that is used in historical fiction is
- ☐ **a.** charts.
- ☐ **b.** dialogue.
- ☐ **c.** accuracy.

5. Historical fiction is probably used most often in
- ☐ **a.** math classes.
- ☐ **b.** science classes.
- ☐ **c.** social studies classes.

Understanding Ideas

1. People who write historical fiction must
- ☐ **a.** do research.
- ☐ **b.** know many languages.
- ☐ **c.** travel to the places they write about.

2. Teachers may use historical novels in their classes because the novels
- ☐ **a.** are less expensive than textbooks.
- ☐ **b.** help bring history "to life" for students.
- ☐ **c.** present facts more accurately than textbooks do.

3. Compared with other types of fiction, historical fiction
- ☐ **a.** has more female characters.
- ☐ **b.** takes place at a specific time in history.
- ☐ **c.** deals with the problems of young people.

4. From the article, you can conclude that
- ☐ **a.** all teachers use historical novels in their classes.
- ☐ **b.** the best books for young people are historical novels.
- ☐ **c.** good historical fiction presents an accurate view of a time period.

5. The author of the article would probably agree that historical fiction
- ☐ **a.** confuses readers.
- ☐ **b.** should replace textbooks.
- ☐ **c.** may help students in social studies classes.

C. Reading Strategies

1. Recognizing Words in Context

Find the word *dramatic* in the article. One definition below is closest to the meaning of that word. One definition has the opposite or nearly the opposite meaning. The remaining definition has a meaning that has nothing to do with the word. Label the definitions **C** for *closest,* **O** for *opposite* or *nearly opposite,* and **U** for *unrelated.*

_____ **a.** related to a specific place
_____ **b.** related to events in real life
_____ **c.** related to the telling of a story

2. Distinguishing Fact from Opinion

Two of the statements below present *facts,* which can be proved. The other statement is an *opinion,* which expresses someone's thoughts or beliefs. Label the statements **F** for *fact* and **O** for *opinion.*

_____ **a.** Authors of historical fiction do a great deal of research.
_____ **b.** Historical fiction is less boring than textbooks.
_____ **c.** Lois Lowry wrote a book called *Number the Stars.*

3. Making Correct Inferences

Two of the statements below are correct *inferences,* or reasonable guesses, that are based on information in the article. The other statement is an incorrect, or faulty, inference. Label the statements **C** for *correct* inference and **I** for *incorrect* inference.

_____ **a.** A story set in the future is not historical fiction.
_____ **b.** People today may face challenges that are similar to the challenges that people faced in the past.
_____ **c.** All historical fiction is written for young people.

4. Understanding Main Ideas

One of the statements below expresses the main idea of the article. Another statement is too general, or too broad. The other explains only part of the article; it is too narrow. Label the statements **M** for *main idea,* **B** for *too broad,* and **N** for *too narrow.*

_____ **a.** Historical fiction stories take place in the past.
_____ **b.** Historical fiction helps students learn about the past through stories.
_____ **c.** Historical fiction uses plot, dialogue, conflict, and other dramatic tools.

5. Responding to the Article

Complete the following sentence in your own words:

Reading "Historical Fiction" made me want to learn more about

____

because ____.

____

D. Expanding Vocabulary

Content-Area Words

Cross out one word in each row that is not related to the word in dark type.

1. **historical**	past	events	new	people
2. **novels**	characters	story	fiction	picture
3. **plot**	story	book	events	match
4. **dialogue**	words	conversation	interest	characters
5. **customs**	readers	traditions	social	cultures

Academic English

In the article "Historical Fiction," you learned that *encounter* means "to face or experience something difficult." *Encounter* can also mean "to meet unexpectedly" or "to come across," as in the following sentence.

I hope that I do not encounter a snake as I walk in the forest.

Complete the sentence below.

1. As Juan walks down the hall at school, he may *encounter* ______________________

Now use the word *encounter* in a sentence of your own.

2. ____

____

You also learned that *contemporary* is an adjective that means "current" or "modern." *Contemporary* can also be a noun that means "someone who lives or lived at the same time as someone else," as in the following sentence.

Tasha's great-grandfather was a contemporary of President Hoover.

Complete the sentence below.

3. I am a *contemporary* of my classmates because ______________________

Now use the word *contemporary* in two sentences of your own.

4. ____

5. ____

Share your new sentences with a partner.

Vocabulary Assessment

Writing a Journal Entry

Read the journal entry. Then complete the sentences. Use words from the Word Bank.

Word Bank
archaeologist
undergo
customs
technology
conflict

Dear Journal,

Today I went to Career Day at my school. We learned about many types of jobs, and now I have an inner (1) ______________—I can't decide what I want to be! I could become an (2) ______________ to study the artifacts and (3) ______________ of ancient people. I could also (4) ______________ training to become an astronaut. It would be fun to learn about the (5) ______________ that makes space missions possible. I'm glad that I have a few more years to decide on a job!

Gabriela

Reading a Newspaper Interview

Read the interview. Circle the word that completes each sentence.

A New Park for Our Neighborhood

by Alex Downing

I had the opportunity to interview Miguel Sanchez, President of the Stonyville Neighborhood (**Association, Elite**).

Downing: Mr. Sanchez, is it true that Stonyville will soon have a new park?

Sanchez: Yes. The park will celebrate the important (**historical, vulgar**) figures of our town, such as the founders and the first mayor.

Downing: I've heard (**novels, rumors**) that the park will be finished by next summer. Is this true?

Sanchez: Unfortunately, the park probably won't be ready for a few more years. We want the park to (**propel, incorporate**) trees, gardens, paths, benches, statues, and a fountain. It will take time to raise money and to build it.

Downing: Can the people of Stonyville do anything to help?

Sanchez: Absolutely! If you want to help, send us your phone number or e-mail address. We will be in (**contact, turmoil**) with you soon!

Making Connections

Work with a partner. Talk about what the words mean. Choose five words and write them in the first column. Write the five remaining words in the second column to create pairs of words that have a connection. In the third column, explain the connection between the words in each pair.

automatic	**retained**	**encounter**	**plot**	**precise**
launched	**missions**	**colonies**	**confusion**	**contemporary**

Word 1	Word 2	Connection

Use all of the words above in a paragraph of your own. Each sentence may include one or more of the words. To help you start writing, look at the connections you wrote about. After you write your paragraph, read it over. If you find a mistake, correct it.

____

____

____

____

____

____

____

Lesson 11

The Storming of the Bastille

Before You Read

Think about what you know. Read the title and the first sentence of the article on the opposite page. What do people do when they storm a building?

Vocabulary

The content-area and academic English words below appear in "The Storming of the Bastille." Read the definitions and the example sentences.

Content-Area Words

infamous (in′fə məs) widely known for bad things
Example: The *infamous* captain of the ship was always mean to his crew.

desperately (des′prit lē) deeply and hopelessly
Example: Many farmers were *desperately* poor during the Great Depression.

arrogant (ar′ə gənt) too proud; believing oneself to be better than others
Example: The *arrogant* dancer liked to brag about her awards.

revolted (ri vōlt′əd) rose up against a government or ruling body
Example: The soldiers *revolted* when the army did not pay them.

legend (lej′ənd) a traditional story that many people believe to be true
Example: One *legend* about George Washington says that he cut down a tree but told the truth about it.

Academic English

rigid (rij′id) strict; not willing or able to change
Example: The school has *rigid* rules about the clothing that students may wear.

revolution (rev′ə lōō′shən) an event that occurs when people fight against an existing government to replace it with a new one
Example: The American colonists fought a *revolution* against Britain to win freedom.

Rate each vocabulary word according to the following scale. Write a number next to each content-area and academic English word.

4 I have never seen the word before.
3 I have seen the word but do not know what it means.
2 I know what the word means when I read it.
1 I use the word myself in speaking or writing.

Now skim the article and look for other words that are new to you. Write each new word and its definition in the Personal Dictionary.

While You Read

Think about why you read. Why was the Bastille an infamous building? How did ordinary French citizens feel about the Bastille? As you read, try to find answers to these questions.

The Storming of the Bastille

The Bastille was an **infamous** building in France. King Charles V built it in 1371 as a castle. Later people used it as a prison. After 1670 it became a jail for people of wealth and high rank who had made the king angry. For more than a century, the Bastille symbolized the cruel power of the king and the wealthy. Several features of the Bastille helped make it very secure. The walls of the structure were 10 feet thick. A moat, or water-filled ditch, surrounded the structure. Heavy guns called *cannons* pointed down from its highest towers.

CONTENT CONNECTION

The French celebrate their national holiday, Bastille Day, on July 14. As you read, think about what this day may mean to the French. What U.S. holiday is similar to Bastille Day? Why?

In the late 1780s, France had a very **rigid,** unfair social system. The common people were **desperately** poor and had little or no chance to make their position better. Meanwhile, the royal family, the upper class, and many church officials were rich. They were also **arrogant.** They believed that they had the right to have an easy life while ordinary people suffered.

The people were ready for a **revolution.** The Enlightenment had started to spread across Europe. This philosophy, or way of thinking, taught that all people had basic rights to life, freedom, and equal treatment. Because of these beliefs, the American colonists had **revolted** against British rule. The colonists won their freedom. The French people acted on the same beliefs. In 1789 the French Revolution began when the common people stormed, or attacked, the Bastille.

LANGUAGE CONNECTION

The idiom *acted on* means "took action because of." What could someone do to act on the belief that nature is important?

In July of 1789, citizens in Paris heard a rumor that alarmed them. The rumor was that troops, or soldiers, were on their way to break up the common people's government. This government was called the *National Assembly*. An angry mob wanted to stop the troops. On July 14, a group of citizens marched through Paris. They marched toward the Bastille because it represented the unfair power that they hated. The crowd shouted, "Down with the Bastille!" They gathered more followers as they marched through the city. When they reached the Bastille, some guards joined them. They managed to cut the chains on a drawbridge. They lowered the drawbridge over the moat. Then the mob ran into the prison. Some people died, but the citizens fought bravely. They battled to gain access to the inside of the jail. After an intense battle, the prison guards gave up the fight. The crowd ran through the jail and released all of the prisoners.

The Bastille contained a supply of arms, or weapons. The citizens took these weapons for themselves. The weapons would help them fight the revolution they had just begun.

One **legend** says that when King Louis XVI heard that the citizens of Paris had stormed the Bastille, he exclaimed, "This is a revolt!" A duke replied, "No, sire, it is a revolution!"

After You Read

A. Organizing Ideas

How did the French Revolution begin? Complete the web below. What are some of the facts that led the citizens of Paris to begin the French Revolution? In each circle, write down one fact. Scan the article to find facts. Some have been done for you.

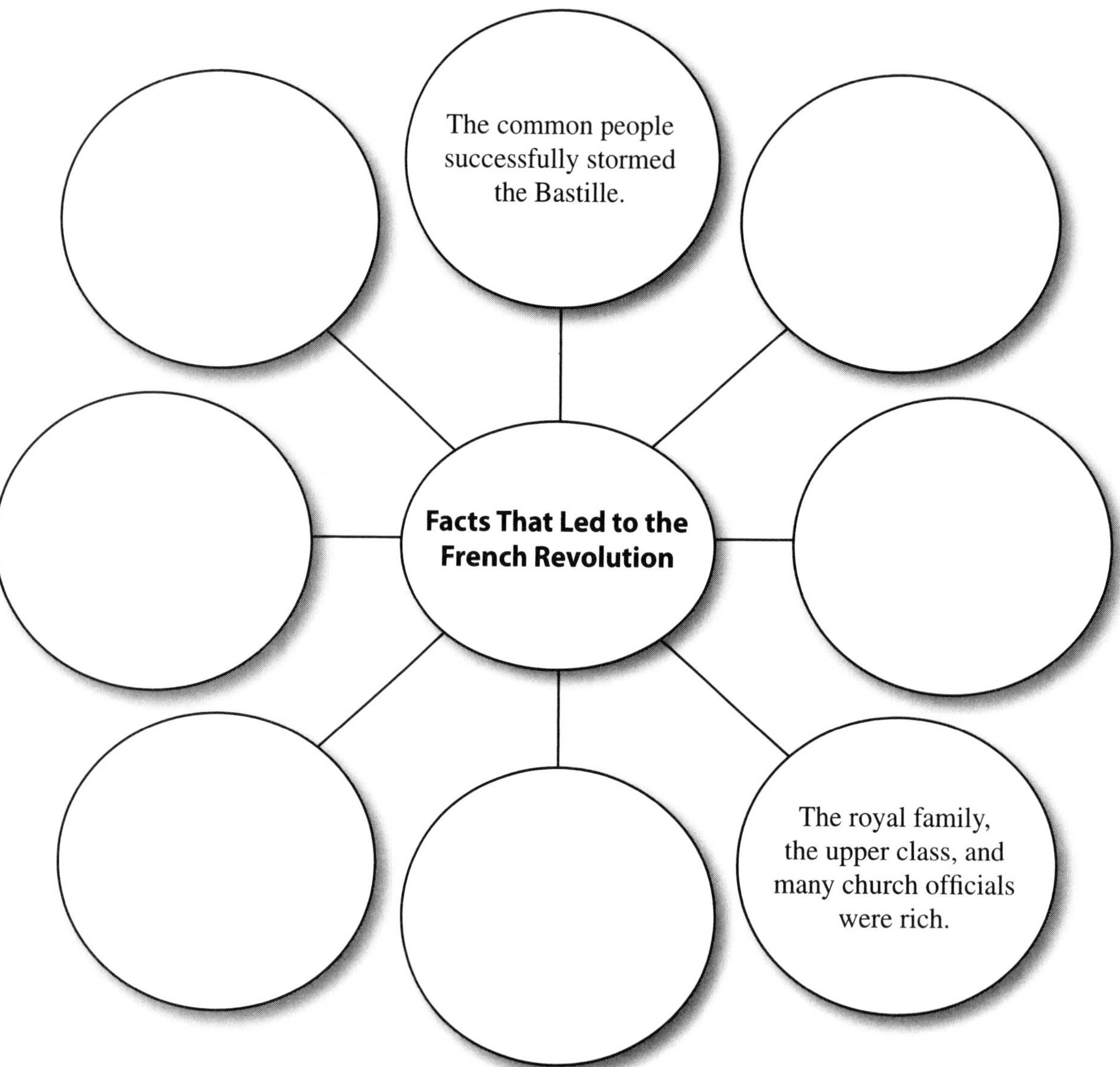

How did completing this web help you better understand why the citizens of Paris revolted? Write two or more sentences to explain your answer. What other way could you have used to organize this information?

____

____

____

B. Comprehension Skills

Tip! **Think about how to find answers.** Look back at different parts of the text. What facts help you figure out how to complete the sentences?

Mark box **a, b,** or **c** with an **X** before the choice that best completes each sentence.

Recalling Facts

1. The Bastille was used as a

- ☐ **a.** prison.
- ☐ **b.** school.
- ☐ **c.** concert hall.

2. The Enlightenment taught that all people

- ☐ **a.** should be wealthy.
- ☐ **b.** have a right to freedom.
- ☐ **c.** should revolt against their government.

3. For the people of France, the Bastille was a symbol of

- ☐ **a.** religion.
- ☐ **b.** unfair power.
- ☐ **c.** foreign power.

4. The citizens of Paris entered the Bastille after they

- ☐ **a.** killed all of the guards.
- ☐ **b.** stole all of the cannons.
- ☐ **c.** cut the chains on a drawbridge.

5. When the citizens of Paris reached the Bastille, they got help from

- ☐ **a.** the royal family.
- ☐ **b.** Enlightenment philosophers.
- ☐ **c.** some guards who joined them.

Understanding Ideas

1. Compared with the upper classes, the common people of France were

- ☐ **a.** extremely poor.
- ☐ **b.** happy with their lives.
- ☐ **c.** philosophical about life.

2. The Enlightenment may have been one cause of the French Revolution, because it taught that

- ☐ **a.** wealth is evil.
- ☐ **b.** people should be able to choose their kings.
- ☐ **c.** all people deserve freedom and equal treatment.

3. The American Revolution

- ☐ **a.** was fought against France.
- ☐ **b.** helped the French decide to revolt.
- ☐ **c.** led to the creation of the National Assembly.

4. It is likely that King Louis XVI

- ☐ **a.** felt sorry for the angry mob.
- ☐ **b.** was not ready to send troops to fight the people.
- ☐ **c.** did not understand the people's hard lives and anger.

5. The author of the article would probably agree that the French citizens

- ☐ **a.** were right to fight for their freedom.
- ☐ **b.** should have had more respect for the king.
- ☐ **c.** should not have battled the guards to storm the Bastille.

C. Reading Strategies

1. Recognizing Words in Context

Find the word *mob* in the article. One definition below is closest to the meaning of that word. One definition has the opposite or nearly the opposite meaning. The remaining definition has a meaning that has nothing to do with the word. Label the definitions **C** for *closest,* **O** for *opposite* or *nearly opposite,* and **U** for *unrelated.*

____ **a.** large crowd of people
____ **b.** single person
____ **c.** government

2. Distinguishing Fact from Opinion

Two of the statements below present *facts,* which can be proved. The other statement is an *opinion,* which expresses someone's thoughts or beliefs. Label the statements **F** for *fact* and **O** for *opinion.*

____ **a.** The king of France did little to improve the lives of the common people.
____ **b.** The citizens of Paris gathered followers as they marched through the city.
____ **c.** The citizens were right to storm the Bastille.

3. Making Correct Inferences

Two of the statements below are correct *inferences,* or reasonable guesses, that are based on information in the article. The other statement is an incorrect, or faulty, inference. Label the statements **C** for *correct* inference and **I** for *incorrect* inference.

____ **a.** The king wanted to have more power than the National Assembly.
____ **b.** The French Revolution took the French many years to plan.
____ **c.** The king and wealthy citizens enjoyed their power.

4. Understanding Main Ideas

One of the statements below expresses the main idea of the article. Another statement is too general, or too broad. The other explains only part of the article; it is too narrow. Label the statements **M** for *main idea,* **B** for *too broad,* and **N** for *too narrow.*

____ **a.** Revolutions have taken place in many nations.
____ **b.** French citizens began a revolution when they stormed the Bastille.
____ **c.** The Enlightenment helped start the French Revolution.

5. Responding to the Article

Complete the following sentence in your own words:
Reading "The Storming of the Bastille" made me want to learn more about

____

because ____

____

D. Expanding Vocabulary

Content-Area Words

Complete each sentence with a word from the box. Write the missing word on the line.

infamous	desperately	arrogant	revolted	legend

1. She was ________________ afraid of the ocean because she could not swim.

2. The peasants ________________ against the king after he forced them to pay high taxes.

3. The "________________ of Sleepy Hollow" tells the story of a headless horseman.

4. The man's terrible crimes made him ________________.

5. I like Duwon, but sometimes he is ________________ about his basketball talent.

Academic English

In the article "The Storming of the Bastille," you learned that *rigid* means "strict" or "not willing or able to change." *Rigid* can also mean "stiff and not bending," as in the following sentence.

Pedro stood rigid with fear as the bee buzzed around his head.

Complete the sentence below.

1. We used a *rigid* pole to ____

Now use the word *rigid* in a sentence of your own.

2. ____

____

You also learned that *revolution* means "an event that involves people who fight against an existing government to replace it with a new one." *Revolution* can also mean "a sudden or extreme change that affects many people and places," as in the following sentence.

The Internet caused a revolution in the way people communicate.

Complete the sentence below.

3. A *revolution* in the way people travel took place when ________________________

Now use the word *revolution* in two sentences of your own.

4. ____

5. ____

Share your new sentences with a partner.

Lesson 12

Franklin Delano Roosevelt's New Deal

Before You Read

Think about what you know. Read the title and the first sentence of each paragraph of the article on the opposite page. What do you predict the article will be about? Why do you think many people consider Franklin Delano Roosevelt to have been one of the greatest U.S. presidents?

Vocabulary

The content-area and academic English words below appear in "Franklin Delano Roosevelt's New Deal." Read the definitions and the example sentences.

Content-Area Words

despite (di spīt′) not prevented by something
Example: Yelena finished the race *despite* the fact that her foot hurt.

stock (stok) part ownership of a company, which people can buy and sell
Example: My grandmother owns *stock* in companies that build airplanes.

Great Depression (grāt di presh′ən) the period in U.S. history from 1929 to 1941, when the economy was poor and many people lost their jobs
Example: During the *Great Depression,* many banks and businesses closed.

insurance (in shoor′əns) protection against risk or loss; a contract that arranges for a person to pay money in exchange for a company's promise to pay money in the case of problems, such as illness or property damage
Example: Maya's *insurance* paid the hospital bills when she broke her arm.

poverty (pov′ər tē) lack of money or possessions
Example: People who live in *poverty* often do not have enough food to eat.

Academic English

contracted (kən trak′tid) became affected by
Example: Saeed *contracted* the flu three times last winter.

confined (kən fīnd′) held within a location
Example: Ben *confined* the puppy to the backyard during the day.

Read again the example sentences that follow the content-area and academic English word definitions. With a partner, discuss the meanings of the words and sentences. Then make up a sentence of your own for each word. Your teacher may wish to discuss your new sentences in class.

Now skim the article and look for other words that are new to you. Write each new word and its definition in the Personal Dictionary.

While You Read

Tip! **Think about why you read.** While Franklin Delano Roosevelt was president, many Americans faced challenges with their money, work, and health. What challenges did Roosevelt face? As you read, look for answers to this question.

Franklin Delano Roosevelt's New Deal

Franklin Delano Roosevelt, whose nickname was FDR, was born in 1882. His family was wealthy. Roosevelt went to the best schools. Then he decided to enter politics. In 1910 he won a seat in the New York State Senate.

Despite his wealth, FDR understood the needs of the common people. He always fought for their rights. After he served a term as secretary of the Navy, he became governor of New York in 1928. At this time, the United States economy was very poor. In 1929 the **stock** market crashed and the **Great Depression** began. Banks and businesses declared bankruptcy, which meant that they had lost all of their money. Millions of people lost their jobs. Roosevelt began new social programs to help the people in the state of New York. He set up unemployment **insurance** for people without jobs. He started pension programs that provided payments to people who had retired from their jobs. He began large public works projects to improve communities. These projects gave people jobs. His social programs in New York helped many people through the hard times. Through his actions, he showed others how these programs could work. In 1932 FDR ran for president as a Democrat. He won the election by a landslide.

Across the country, the Depression had become worse. **Poverty** was everywhere. As president, Roosevelt created national programs similar to the programs he had started in New York. He called these programs a "New Deal" for America. He got Congress to pass laws that paid relief money to poor people and to farmers. The New Deal included programs that provided jobs for many unemployed people. The Works Progress Administration was a program that hired workers to build bridges and roads. Workers also planted trees and did other work to help the country. FDR also set up a new type of insurance to protect the savings that people kept in banks. As a result, people gained new faith in banks. They began to have more hope for the future. The programs did a great deal to help lift the country out of the Depression.

Many people consider FDR to have been one of the greatest presidents ever. He showed great care and commitment in his fight to help the common people. He was brilliant and full of life, despite the fact that he had **contracted** a disease called *polio* when he was 39 years old. During much of his presidency, the disease **confined** him to a wheelchair. However, his disability never affected his fight for a good life for all Americans.

LANGUAGE CONNECTION

A nickname is a shorter form of a name that many people use to refer to a person. Franklin Delano Roosevelt's nickname was his initials: FDR. What famous people of today have nicknames? Do you have a nickname?

CONTENT CONNECTION

When FDR was president, the radio was becoming popular. FDR used the radio to give a series of 30 radio talks—his famous "fireside chats"—to the American people. Listeners felt that FDR was right there in their homes as he explained the New Deal programs and gave them hope during difficult times. How does the U.S. president talk to the American people today?

After You Read

A. Organizing Ideas

What made FDR a great leader during the Depression? Complete the organizer below. First think about the main idea of the article. Then look back at the article to find facts that support the main idea. In the boxes, write the facts in complete sentences. One has been done for you.

Main Idea: FDR helped people during one of the worst challenges in U.S. history.

↓

↓

↓

FDR created programs that paid relief money to poor people and to farmers.

↓

↓

↓

How would you describe FDR? Write two or more sentences to explain your answer. How did the organizer help you describe him?

B. Comprehension Skills

Tip! **Think about how to find answers.** Read each sentence below. Underline the words that will help you figure out how to complete each item.

Mark box **a, b,** or **c** with an **X** before the choice that best completes each sentence.

Recalling Facts

1. FDR grew up in a family that
- ☐ **a.** was wealthy.
- ☐ **b.** was unknown.
- ☐ **c.** had little money.

2. Just before FDR became president, he was
- ☐ **a.** a U.S. senator.
- ☐ **b.** the secretary of the Navy.
- ☐ **c.** the governor of New York.

3. The Great Depression began in
- ☐ **a.** 1910.
- ☐ **b.** 1921.
- ☐ **c.** 1929.

4. FDR began his social programs in response to
- ☐ **a.** the New Deal.
- ☐ **b.** the Great Depression.
- ☐ **c.** the Works Progress Administration.

5. FDR suffered from
- ☐ **a.** polio.
- ☐ **b.** poverty.
- ☐ **c.** depression.

Understanding Ideas

1. From the article, you can conclude that before FDR was president, banks
- ☐ **a.** did not pay interest on people's savings.
- ☐ **b.** did not provide insurance for people's savings.
- ☐ **c.** did not allow ordinary people to have savings accounts.

2. You can also conclude that FDR's main goal was to
- ☐ **a.** help people escape poverty.
- ☐ **b.** serve more than one term as president.
- ☐ **c.** make sure that banks stayed in business.

3. The social programs that FDR created as governor and as president both
- ☐ **a.** involved insurance for banks.
- ☐ **b.** improved the U.S. Navy.
- ☐ **c.** put people back to work.

4. FDR's public works projects helped relieve poverty because
- ☐ **a.** they provided jobs for people.
- ☐ **b.** roads helped people get to jobs.
- ☐ **c.** they gave money to poor people and to farmers.

5. The author of the article would probably agree that
- ☐ **a.** FDR favored rich people.
- ☐ **b.** FDR was an exceptional leader.
- ☐ **c.** FDR was too rich to understand ordinary people.

C. Reading Strategies

1. Recognizing Words in Context

Find the word *landslide* in the article. One definition below is closest to the meaning of that word. One definition has the opposite or nearly the opposite meaning. The remaining definition has a meaning that has nothing to do with the word. Label the definitions **C** for *closest,* **O** for *opposite* or *nearly opposite,* and **U** for *unrelated.*

_____ **a.** an unexpected event
_____ **b.** a huge win
_____ **c.** a close election

2. Distinguishing Fact from Opinion

Two of the statements below present *facts,* which can be proved. The other statement is an *opinion,* which expresses someone's thoughts or beliefs. Label the statements **F** for *fact* and **O** for *opinion.*

_____ **a.** FDR was the greatest president in U.S. history.
_____ **b.** FDR helped the United States fight the Great Depression.
_____ **c.** FDR grew up in a wealthy family.

3. Making Correct Inferences

Two of the statements below are correct *inferences,* or reasonable guesses, that are based on information in the article. The other statement is an incorrect, or faulty, inference. Label the statements **C** for *correct* inference and **I** for *incorrect* inference.

_____ **a.** When banks declared bankruptcy, people lost their savings.
_____ **b.** FDR suffered from polio when he was governor of New York.
_____ **c.** Congress did not want to pass laws to pay relief money to poor people.

4. Understanding Main Ideas

One of the statements below expresses the main idea of the article. Another statement is too general, or too broad. The other explains only part of the article; it is too narrow. Label the statements **M** for *main idea,* **B** for *too broad,* and **N** for *too narrow.*

_____ **a.** FDR served as president during the Great Depression.
_____ **b.** FDR set up insurance that helped people trust banks again.
_____ **c.** FDR created programs that helped people during the Great Depression.

5. Responding to the Article

Complete the following sentence in your own words:

Before reading "Franklin Delano Roosevelt's New Deal," I already knew

____

____

D. Expanding Vocabulary

Content-Area Words

Read each item carefully. Write on the line the word or phrase that best completes each sentence.

1. People may live in poverty if they __________________.
   feel tired | cannot find jobs | own a house
2. Olena smiled despite the fact that she felt __________________.
   sad | happy | excited
3. A person who owns stock in a company hopes that the company __________________.
   fails | hires new workers | does well
4. People often buy insurance to protect their __________________.
   homes | lawns | president
5. During the Great Depression, many people __________________.
   earned high wages | left the country | felt hopeless

Academic English

In the article "Franklin Delano Roosevelt's New Deal," you learned that *contracted* means "became affected by." *Contracted* (kon′trakt əd) can also mean "set up a contract, or legal agreement," as in the following sentence.

The school contracted with a carpenter to build a new fence.

Complete the sentence below.

1. Mr. Delmar *contracted* with an architect to ____________________________________

Now use the word *contracted* in a sentence of your own.

2. ____
   ____

You also learned that *confined* means "held within a location." *Confined* can also mean "kept within limits," as in the following sentence.

The guest list for Lin's party was confined to 10 friends.

Complete the sentence below.

3. The president *confined* his speech to ____

Now use the word *confined* in two sentences of your own.

4. ____
5. ____

Share your new sentences with a partner.

Photojournalism: Stories in Pictures

Before You Read

Think about what you know. Read the lesson title above. Have you ever seen a group of pictures that told a story about an event? Has a picture ever caused you to feel happy or sad?

Vocabulary

The content-area and academic English words below appear in "Photojournalism: Stories in Pictures." Read the definitions and the example sentences.

Content-Area Words

potent (pōt′ənt) strong; powerful
Example: This drink has a *potent* berry flavor.

present (prez′ənt) in a particular place at a certain time
Example: Larisa was not *present* to pick up her award after the contest.

guilty (gil′tē) responsible for a wrong action that deserves punishment
Example: The prisoners were *guilty* of the bank robbery.

defendants (di fen′dənts) people who go on trial before a judge because they may have broken a law
Example: The *defendants* told the judge that they did not steal the car.

conveys (kən vāz′) expresses; communicates
Example: This song *conveys* my feelings about friendship.

Academic English

promote (prə mōt′) to try to sell something or make people like something
Example: The television ads *promote* the new movie.

publish (pub′lish) to put into printed form to give or sell to the public
Example: Sari plans to *publish* her poems in the school magazine.

Do any of the words above seem related? Sort the seven vocabulary words into two or more categories. Write the words down on note cards or in a chart. Words may fit into more than one group. You may wish to work with a partner for this activity.

Now skim the article and look for other words that are new to you. Write each new word and its definition in the Personal Dictionary.

While You Read

Tip! **Think about why you read.** What is it like to be a photojournalist? Write down a question about this career that you would like to know the answer to. As you read, try to find the answer.

Photojournalism
Stories in Pictures

Photographs are everywhere. They decorate the walls of homes. Stores use them to **promote** everything from food to clothes to cars. The news contains pictures of fires and floods, special events, and famous faces. Photos record the beautiful sights of nature. They also allow people to see things that are far away. Through photos, people can see wild animals, cities in foreign lands, and even the stars in outer space. Photos also tell stories.

People who work in photojournalism report the news through photos. Sometimes photojournalists tell stories through a single picture. At other times they use a group of pictures, called a *photo essay,* to tell a story. Each picture is like a chapter in a book. A photo essay can do more than share facts. It can also be a **potent** force for social change.

Jacob Riis was one of the first photojournalists. He took pictures of parts of New York City where poor people lived. Riis believed that poverty caused crime, and he used photos to help him prove this point. A few years later, Lewis Hine took photographs that shocked the public. The photos showed small children at work in factories. Hine's pictures helped people decide to write laws to protect children from unfair labor.

Photojournalists try to be **present** at important events. For example, President Abraham Lincoln was killed in 1865. People wanted to know more about the people who were **guilty** of this crime. Alexander Gardner took pictures of the **defendants** when they came to trial and received punishment.

Photojournalists may have to take hundreds of pictures in order to get one or two really good photos. They must combine science and art to make successful pictures. They use science to make the photo come out clearly, instead of blurry or too dark or too light. They use art to make a photo that has a good design and that **conveys** feeling. Photojournalists make a factual, or true, record of what they see. However, a photo can be both a work of art and a factual record. It can show an important event through a beautiful image, or through an image that touches people's feelings.

As historical and artistic documents, photos can become more important over time. Today photojournalists still take pictures for newspapers and magazines. They also **publish** their pictures in books and on the Internet.

LANGUAGE CONNECTION

A simile uses *like* or *as* to compare two different objects or ideas. Explain what the simile *each picture is like a chapter in a book* means.

CONTENT CONNECTION

Dorothea Lange was a photojournalist during the Great Depression. One of her most famous photos shows a farm family that looks desperately poor, sad, and hungry. People who saw the photo understood how terrible the Great Depression was for farmworkers. What photo has influenced you in some way?

After You Read

A. Organizing Ideas

What do you know about photojournalism? Complete the organizer below. Read the questions in the circles, and then record your answers in the squares. Refer to the article for help. One answer has been done for you.

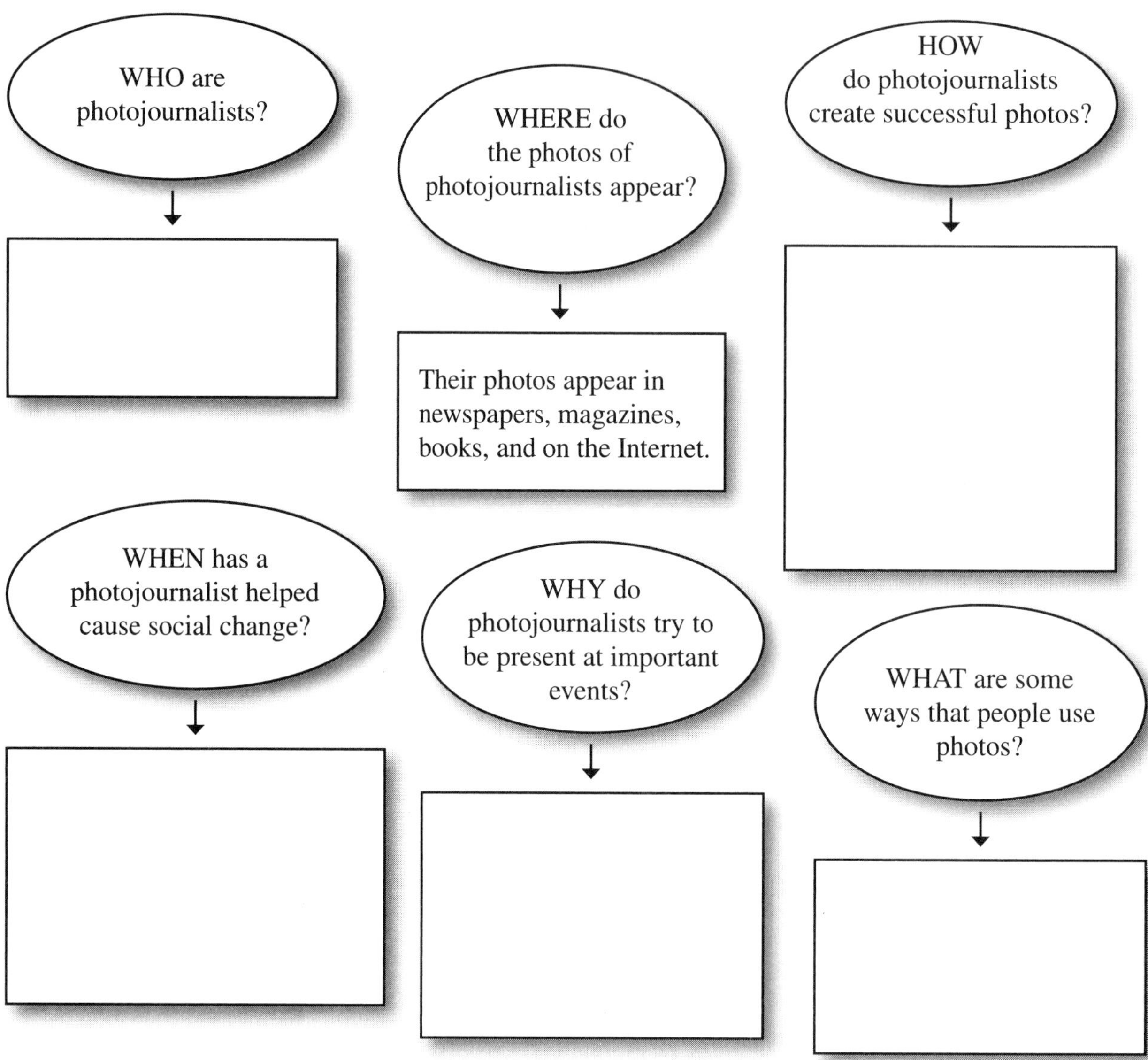

How did answering the questions help you understand the article? What do you find most interesting about photojournalism? Write two or more sentences to answer these questions. Would you use this type of organizer again? Why or why not?

____

____

____

B. Comprehension Skills

 **Think about how to find answers.** Think about what each sentence means. Try to say it to yourself in your own words before you complete it.

Mark box **a, b,** or **c** with an **X** before the choice that best completes each sentence.

Recalling Facts

1. A photojournalist is a person who
- ☐ **a.** makes works of art.
- ☐ **b.** writes news articles.
- ☐ **c.** reports the news through photos.

2. A photo essay is
- ☐ **a.** a book about photography.
- ☐ **b.** a group of photos that tells a story.
- ☐ **c.** a photo that helps people understand an essay.

3. Photojournalist Jacob Riis took pictures of
- ☐ **a.** small children at work in factories.
- ☐ **b.** parts of New York City where poor people lived.
- ☐ **c.** the people on trial for the death of President Lincoln.

4. To get one good photo, photojournalists
- ☐ **a.** may take hundreds of pictures.
- ☐ **b.** ask the people in the picture to sit very still.
- ☐ **c** take pictures only of beautiful people and places.

5. Today photojournalists put their pictures
- ☐ **a.** only in magazines.
- ☐ **b.** in books instead of newspapers.
- ☐ **c.** on the Internet as well as in newspapers, magazines, and books.

Understanding Ideas

1. The author would probably agree that
- ☐ **a.** all photos are works of art.
- ☐ **b.** the best photojournalists have both science and art skills.
- ☐ **c.** only trained artists should take photos for the public to see.

2. Many people did not know that small children worked in factories
- ☐ **a.** because they did not care.
- ☐ **b.** until they saw photos of the children at work.
- ☐ **c.** until the children told them.

3. Photos in a photo essay are like chapters in a book because
- ☐ **a.** writers make up the story.
- ☐ **b.** some books have pictures.
- ☐ **c.** each picture tells part of a story.

4. Photojournalists probably work
- ☐ **a.** slowly, so that each picture will be perfect.
- ☐ **b.** only when something important happens.
- ☐ **c.** quickly, so that they will have many pictures to choose from.

5. The main idea of the article is that
- ☐ **a.** photojournalists tell the news through photos.
- ☐ **b.** photos allow people to see things that are far away.
- ☐ **c.** photojournalists are also artists.

C. Reading Strategies

1. Recognizing Words in Context

Find the word *shocked* in the article. One definition below is closest to the meaning of that word. One definition has the opposite or nearly the opposite meaning. The remaining definition has a meaning that has nothing to do with the word. Label the definitions **C** for *closest,* **O** for *opposite* or *nearly opposite,* and **U** for *unrelated.*

_____ **a.** surprised
_____ **b.** bored
_____ **c.** approached

2. Distinguishing Fact from Opinion

Two of the statements below present *facts,* which can be proved. The other statement is an *opinion,* which expresses someone's thoughts or beliefs. Label the statements **F** for *fact* and **O** for *opinion.*

_____ **a.** Jacob Riis showed poverty in New York City with his photos.
_____ **b.** Photojournalism involves both science and art.
_____ **c.** Photos are more important than words in news stories.

3. Making Correct Inferences

Two of the statements below are correct *inferences,* or reasonable guesses, that are based on information in the article. The other statement is an incorrect, or faulty, inference. Label the statements **C** for *correct* inference and **I** for *incorrect* inference.

_____ **a.** It is difficult to take a photo that is good enough to be in a newspaper.
_____ **b.** Factories hired Lewis Hine to take photos.
_____ **c.** Photos often appeal to people's emotions.

4. Understanding Main Ideas

One of the statements below expresses the main idea of the article. Another statement is too general, or too broad. The other explains only part of the article; it is too narrow. Label the statements **M** for *main idea,* **B** for *too broad,* and **N** for *too narrow.*

_____ **a.** Photojournalism tells the news through pictures.
_____ **b.** People use photographs in many different ways.
_____ **c.** Photojournalists can help create social change through photo essays.

5. Responding to the Article

Complete the following sentences in your own words:

One of the things I did best while reading "Photojournalism: Stories in Pictures" was

____

I think that I did this well because ____

____

D. Expanding Vocabulary

Content-Area Words

Cross out one word in each row that is not related to the word in dark type.

1. potent	strong	artistic	force	powerful
2. present	document	time	attend	place
3. guilty	wrong	punish	judge	report
4. defendants	judge	design	trial	crime
5. conveys	shows	expresses	records	communicates

Academic English

In the article "Photojournalism: Stories in Pictures," you learned that *promote* means "to try to sell something or make people like something." *Promote* can also mean "to help with the growth, development, or progress of something," as in the following sentence.

Foods that contain vitamins promote good health.

Complete the sentence below.

1. A person can *promote* healthy teeth by ______________________________

Now use the word *promote* in a sentence of your own.

2. ______________________________

____

You also learned that *publish* means "to put into printed form to give or sell to the public." *Publish* can also mean "to make something known to the public," as in the following sentence.

The judge will not publish the names of people who give information about crimes.

Complete the sentence below.

3. Next week the school will *publish* the results of ______________________________

Now use the word *publish* in two sentences of your own.

4. ______________________________

5. ______________________________

Share your new sentences with a partner.

Lesson 14

What Are a Mayor's Responsibilities?

Before You Read

Think about what you know. Read the lesson title above. What do you predict the article will be about? What do you already know about the work a mayor does?

Vocabulary

The content-area and academic English words below appear in "What Are a Mayor's Responsibilities?" Read the definitions and the example sentences.

Content-Area Words

councils (koun′səlz) groups of people that citizens elect to make decisions and laws for a city
Example: Town *councils* in the area met to talk about a clean water project.

budget (buj′it) a plan for how to spend money on different things
Example: Chun's *budget* shows that he will spend $100 on lunch each month.

executive (ig zek′yə tiv) a person who directs or manages a company or a government
Example: The company *executive* decided to pay the workers more.

efficiently (i fish′ənt lē) with as little effort or waste as possible
Example: The family divided the chores to clean the house *efficiently*.

consumer (kən so͞o′mər) someone who buys or uses a product
Example: A *consumer* may return an item to the store if it does not work.

Academic English

functions (fungk′shənz) operates; works
Example: A car *functions* best when the owner takes good care of it.

environment (en vī′rən mənt) all things that may affect the ability of people, animals, and plants to survive and grow
Example: When the *environment* is healthy, people have clean air to breathe.

Complete the sentences below that contain the content-area and academic English words above. Use the spaces provided. The first one has been done for you.

1. A school *budget* may include money for sports equipment.
2. We traveled *efficiently* by ______________.
3. A careful *consumer* would compare ______________.
4. A city *executive* makes decisions about ______________.
5. One animal that lives in a cold *environment* is ______________.
6. A heart that *functions* properly pumps ______________.
7. The two city *councils* met to discuss ______________.

Now skim the article and look for other words that are new to you. Write each new word and its definition in the Personal Dictionary.

While You Read

Think about why you read. How may a mayor affect the lives of the citizens in a city? As you read, try to find answers to this question.

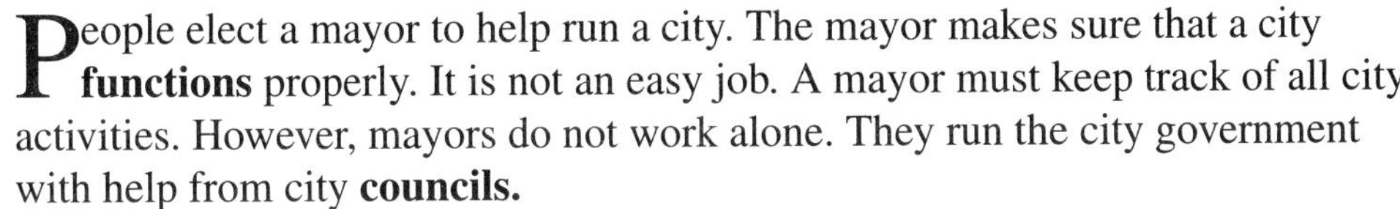

What Are a Mayor's Responsibilities?

People elect a mayor to help run a city. The mayor makes sure that a city **functions** properly. It is not an easy job. A mayor must keep track of all city activities. However, mayors do not work alone. They run the city government with help from city **councils.**

Mayors may be "weak" or "strong." In cities that use a weak-mayor system, the city council has most of the power. The council prepares the city **budget.** It hires and fires city employees, or workers. Under this system, people elect the council members and the leaders of some departments, or city offices. The council also may choose leaders for city departments. A city may have many boards and committees, which are groups that make decisions. Each group manages one city department. Although people elect the mayor, he or she has little power. The weak mayor may suggest leaders for city departments. However, the council must approve these suggestions. In most cases, the mayor cannot veto, or override, a council decision.

In a strong-mayor system, the elected mayor is the city's main **executive.** The mayor chooses the leaders of each department. He or she makes sure that these leaders run their departments **efficiently.** The elected city council does not have the power to approve the leaders that the mayor chooses. The council cannot veto a decision that the mayor makes. However, the mayor has the right to veto decisions that the council makes.

Strong mayors check the work of many different city departments. These departments include fire, police, health, and transportation. Some mayors may check the work of a city-planning department. This department plans the way that the city will grow and develop. In a large city, such as New York, the mayor may also check the work of other departments. These departments could include culture, prisons, parks, **consumer** issues, immigration, and **environment.** New York's mayor also chooses judges for the city courts. The mayor makes sure that people who break the laws are punished.

A strong mayor prepares the city budget. In this sense, the mayor decides how to spend money for city services. Citizens know whom to blame if services fail. However, the mayor works with the council to figure out the needs of the city and to complete city projects.

Strong mayors have a great deal of control over the government of a city. However, they must stay within the law. Most cities have a written city charter that explains city laws and tells how the city and its departments should be organized. The charter also explains the duties of the mayor and other officials.

LANGUAGE CONNECTION

Sometimes a noun may act as an adjective. In the phrase *city government,* the noun *city* acts as an adjective. *City* describes one type of government. In the first paragraph, does *city* act as an adjective in *city functions* or in *city councils?*

CONTENT CONNECTION

Does your city have a law that says people must wear helmets when they ride bikes? If you are not sure, how could you find out? Write down one question you have about the laws in your city. Who could you talk to if you wanted a law to change?

After You Read

A. Organizing Ideas

How are weak-mayor and strong-mayor systems similar and different? Complete the diagram below. In the left circle, list facts about weak-mayor systems. In the right circle, list facts about strong-mayor systems. In the section where the two circles overlap, list facts that apply to both weak-mayor and strong-mayor systems. Refer to the article for help. Some have been done for you.

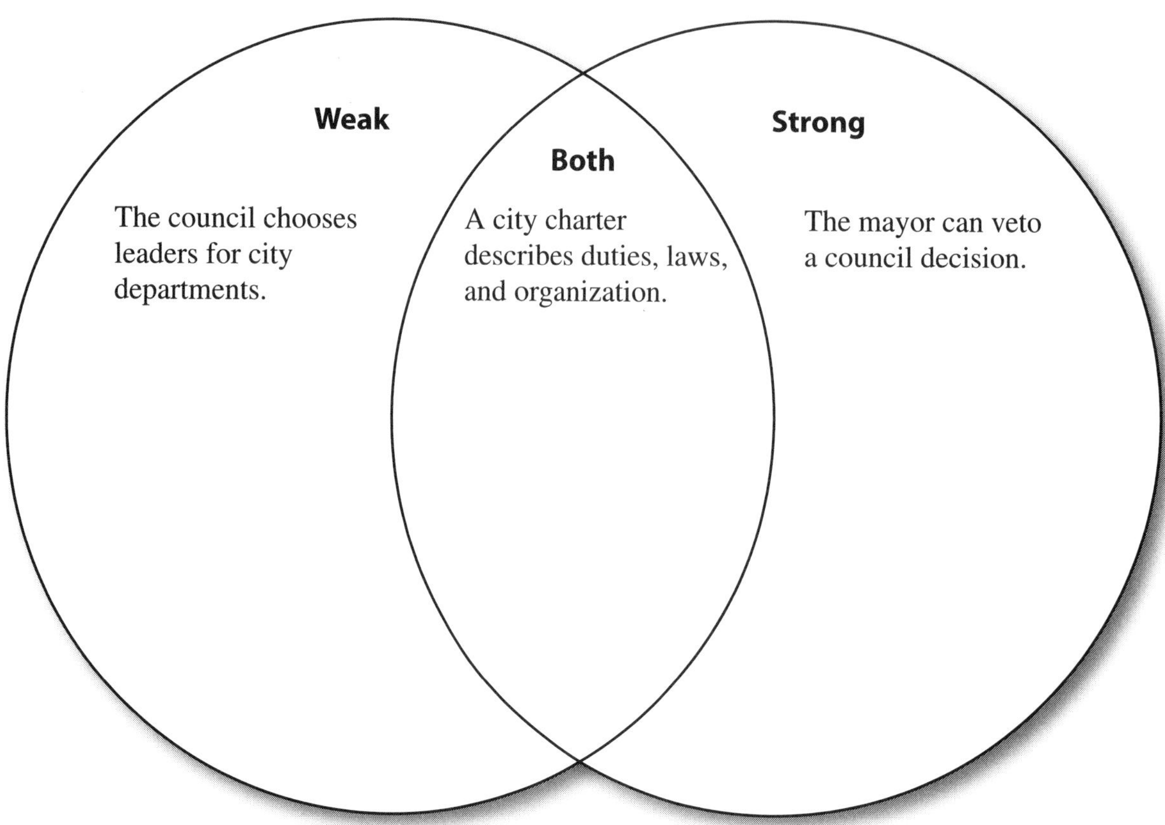

How did completing this diagram help you compare strong mayors and weak mayors? Write two or more sentences to answer this question. In what other way could you have organized this information?

____

____

____

____

____

____

B. Comprehension Skills

Think about how to find answers. Look back at what you read. The information is in the text, but you may have to look in several sentences to find it.

Mark box **a, b,** or **c** with an **X** before the choice that best completes each sentence.

Recalling Facts

1. The mayor of a city is elected by
- ☐ **a.** citizens.
- ☐ **b.** the city council.
- ☐ **c.** department leaders.

2. Weak mayors do not always have
- ☐ **a.** employees.
- ☐ **b.** city councils.
- ☐ **c.** the right to veto a council decision.

3. A city budget contains information about how to
- ☐ **a.** raise taxes.
- ☐ **b.** hire and fire city workers.
- ☐ **c.** spend money on city services.

4. In cities with weak mayors, most decisions are made by
- ☐ **a.** a strong mayor.
- ☐ **b.** the city council.
- ☐ **c** department leaders.

5. The power of a strong mayor is limited by
- ☐ **a.** the city charter.
- ☐ **b.** the veto of the city council.
- ☐ **c.** the city-planning department.

Understanding Ideas

1. A strong mayor is likely to check
- ☐ **a.** the decisions that judges make.
- ☐ **b.** the work done to improve roads.
- ☐ **c.** the money that the city gets from the state.

2. One difference between strong mayors and weak mayors is that
- ☐ **a.** weak mayors are not elected.
- ☐ **b.** strong mayors prepare the city budget.
- ☐ **c.** the cities of weak mayors do not have charters.

3. If city services fail in a city with a strong-mayor system, citizens probably will
- ☐ **a.** not elect the same mayor again.
- ☐ **b.** demand changes to the city charter.
- ☐ **c.** fire the leaders of city departments.

4. The author of the article would probably agree that
- ☐ **a.** mayors have a challenging job.
- ☐ **b.** states give cities too little money.
- ☐ **c.** a weak mayor of a small city has little to do.

5. If a weak mayor chooses a department leader but that person does not become the leader, it is probably because
- ☐ **a.** the department no longer exists.
- ☐ **b.** the city council has vetoed the mayor's decision.
- ☐ **c.** the city council has not given the department enough money.

C. Reading Strategies

1. Recognizing Words in Context

Find the word *veto* in the article. One definition below is closest to the meaning of that word. One definition has the opposite or nearly the opposite meaning. The remaining definition has a meaning that has nothing to do with the word. Label the definitions **C** for *closest,* **O** for *opposite* or *nearly opposite,* and **U** for *unrelated.*

_____ **a.** vote for
_____ **b.** vote against
_____ **c.** refuse to vote

2. Distinguishing Fact from Opinion

Two of the statements below present *facts,* which can be proved. The other statement is an *opinion,* which expresses someone's thoughts or beliefs. Label the statements **F** for *fact* and **O** for *opinion.*

_____ **a.** Strong mayors have more power than weak mayors do.
_____ **b.** Strong mayors are better at their jobs than weak mayors are.
_____ **c.** Citizens elect the members of a city council.

3. Making Correct Inferences

Two of the statements below are correct *inferences,* or reasonable guesses, that are based on information in the article. The other statement is an incorrect, or faulty, inference. Label the statements **C** for *correct* inference and **I** for *incorrect* inference.

_____ **a.** In a strong-mayor system, the city council is likely to choose a department leader that the mayor does not approve of.
_____ **b.** All mayors are elected by citizens.
_____ **c.** Large cities often have more departments than small cities do.

4. Understanding Main Ideas

One of the statements below expresses the main idea of the article. Another statement is too general, or too broad. The other explains only part of the article; it is too narrow. Label the statements **M** for *main idea,* **B** for *too broad,* and **N** for *too narrow.*

_____ **a.** Mayors work to make sure that a city functions properly.
_____ **b.** The power that a mayor has depends on the system.
_____ **c.** A written city charter often explains city laws.

5. Responding to the Article

Complete the following sentence in your own words:
From reading "What Are a Mayor's Responsibilities?" I have learned

____

____

D. Expanding Vocabulary

Content-Area Words

Complete each sentence with a word from the box. Write the missing word on the line.

councils	budget	executive	efficiently	consumer

1. The company ________________ makes the final decisions about whom to hire.
2. Mrs. Xiong has worked on the ________________ of many different cities.
3. Danilo is a regular ________________ of candy bars.
4. A fire in a fireplace does not heat a home very ________________.
5. The money for a new bike is not in my ________________.

Academic English

In the article "What Are a Mayor's Responsibilities?" you learned that *functions* means "operates" or "works." *Functions* can also mean "performs the job of something else" or "serves as," as in the following sentence.

In spring, the football field functions as a place for people to fly kites.

Complete the sentence below.

1. My chair *functions* as a stool when ________________________________

Now use the word *functions* in a sentence of your own.

2. ____

____

You also learned that *environment* means "all things that may affect the ability of people, animals, and plants to survive and grow." *Environment* can also mean "the things that surround someone," as in the following sentence.

Rana needs a quiet environment to study for her test.

Complete the sentence below.

3. To create a fun *environment* for the students, the teacher ________________________

Now use the word *environment* in two sentences of your own.

4. ____
5. ____

Share your new sentences with a partner.

Lesson 15 The Plains Indians and the Buffalo

Before You Read

Think about what you know. Read the title and the first paragraph of the article on the opposite page. Think of an animal that is an important symbol in U.S. culture or in your home culture. Why is the animal an important symbol?

Vocabulary

The content-area and academic English words below appear in "The Plains Indians and the Buffalo." Read the definitions and the example sentences.

Content-Area Words

vital (vīt′əl) necessary for life

Example: Water is *vital* to the survival of people, animals, and plants.

sacred (sā′krid) worthy of religious respect

Example: Ancient people believed that things in nature, such as rivers, were *sacred*.

ceremonies (ser′ə mō′nēz) traditional events that follow a pattern or set of rules

Example: Wedding *ceremonies* take place when people get married.

grease (grēs) a thick, oily liquid that makes materials more slippery or smooth

Example: Akiko rubbed *grease* on her bike chain to make it turn more easily.

role (rōl) a part that someone or something plays

Example: My friend plays the *role* of the queen in our high school play.

Academic English

prime (prīm) first in rank or importance

Example: Cold weather was the *prime* reason that the tomatoes did not grow well.

assured (ə shoord′) made certain

Example: The leaders signed an agreement that *assured* that the war was over.

Answer the questions below about the content-area and academic English words. Write your answers in the spaces provided. The first one has been done for you.

1. What word goes with *most important?* ___prime___
2. What word goes with *religious events that follow steps?* ______________
3. What word goes with *slippery liquid?* ______________
4. What word goes with *made sure that something will happen?* ______________
5. What word goes with *honored for religious importance?* ______________
6. What word goes with *part that an actor plays in a movie?* ______________
7. What word goes with *completely necessary?* ______________

Now skim the article and look for other words that are new to you. Write each new word and its definition in the Personal Dictionary.

While You Read

Tip! **Think about why you read.** The Plains Indians used every part of the buffalo they killed. Write down some of the parts of a buffalo. As you read, look for ways that the Plains Indians used these parts.

The Plains Indians and the Buffalo

Many Native Americans live in the United States. Several groups of Plains Indians live in the Great Plains region. Three of these groups are the Sioux, the Cheyenne, and the Arapaho. The bison, or buffalo, is very important in the culture of the Plains Indians. The buffalo was once their most **vital** resource, or source of materials. It was also part of the Native religions. The Plains Indians believed that the buffalo was **sacred.** They respected the animal because it provided clothes and food for them. The buffalo was also a symbol of inner strength. It reminded the people that all creatures depend on one another to survive.

The Plains Indians hunted many animals. However, the buffalo was of **prime** importance to them. They never killed more buffalo than they needed. They tracked the movements of the animals. They performed special songs and dances when they saw a herd. The dancers wore masks of an entire buffalo head. After these **ceremonies,** the warriors began the hunt. They usually hunted the buffalo on horseback, or on horses. The men used bows and arrows. While the men hunted, the women set up the camp. Once the hunters killed a buffalo, the women and children helped carry it back to camp.

The people did not waste any part of the buffalo. They used the meat for food. They could dry the meat to keep it for a long time. They used the skin to make clothes, blankets, and tentlike homes called *tepees*. They also stretched buffalo skin to make boats. They made spoons and cups from buffalo horns, and they made tools from buffalo bones. They cleaned the stomach and intestines of the buffalo and used them as containers to carry water. They boiled buffalo hooves to make glue. Buffalo sinew, which people got from the muscles of the backbone, served as sewing thread. People also used sinew to make shoes to walk on snow. Buffalo teeth became ornaments, or decorations, on jewelry. Women made soap, candles, and hair **grease** from the buffalo fat. The fur from the buffalo beard decorated clothes. People used the tail as a flyswatter or as a whip.

The buffalo skull, or head bones, played an important **role** in religious ceremonies. It served as an altar, or a place for religious activities. People brought symbols of their worship to it. They stuffed the eyes and nose of the skull with grass to symbolize vegetation, or plant life. If the land had enough vegetation, the buffalo would be healthy. Healthy buffalo **assured** that the people would have enough to eat.

CONTENT CONNECTION

During the 1800s, buffalo almost became extinct. This means that almost all of the buffalo died. Eventually the government moved the buffalo that were left to Yellowstone National Park to protect them. What animals do you know of that are almost extinct? What can people do to help save them?

LANGUAGE CONNECTION

Hooves and *teeth* are plural nouns, which means that they refer to more than one object. Singular nouns refer to just one object. What are the singular forms of *hooves* and *teeth?*

After You Read

A. Organizing Ideas

How were buffalo important to the Plains Indians? Draw a buffalo in the space below. Label each part of the animal. Use all of the words in the box below. Next to each label, write down how the Plains Indians used the part. For example, next to "stomach and intestines," write "water containers." Refer to the article for information.

meat	**fat**	**hooves**	**skin**	**horns**	**skull**
teeth	**sinew**	**beard**	**tail**	**stomach and intestines**	

How would you describe the way of life of the Plains Indians? Write two or more sentences to answer this question. How did your drawing help you answer the question? Would you use a drawing again to help you organize ideas?

____

____

____

____

____

B. Comprehension Skills

Tip! **Think about how to find answers.** Look back at what you read. The words in an answer are usually contained in a single sentence.

Mark box **a, b,** or **c** with an **X** before the choice that best completes each sentence.

Recalling Facts

1. One of the Plains Indians groups is the
- ☐ **a.** Sioux.
- ☐ **b.** Navajo.
- ☐ **c.** Cherokee.

2. The buffalo was a symbol of
- ☐ **a.** peace.
- ☐ **b.** freedom.
- ☐ **c.** inner strength.

3. People used buffalo bones to make
- ☐ **a.** tools.
- ☐ **b.** whips.
- ☐ **c.** candles.

4. In religious ceremonies, people used the buffalo
- ☐ **a.** tail.
- ☐ **b.** skull.
- ☐ **c.** hooves.

5. Sinew comes from buffalo
- ☐ **a.** teeth.
- ☐ **b.** bones.
- ☐ **c.** muscles.

Understanding Ideas

1. The buffalo was important in the religions of the Plains Indians because
- ☐ **a.** it was so huge.
- ☐ **b.** dancers wore buffalo head masks.
- ☐ **c.** it was important for their survival.

2. When the Plains Indians could not find buffalo to hunt, they probably
- ☐ **a.** suffered hard times.
- ☐ **b.** blamed their religion.
- ☐ **c.** noticed nothing different.

3. It is most likely true that
- ☐ **a.** people in the United States still commonly use buffalo for food and clothing.
- ☐ **b.** when buffalo herds began to disappear, the Plains Indians had to change their way of life.
- ☐ **c.** the buffalo is more important to the Plains Indians now than it used to be.

4. From the article, you can conclude that the Plains Indians
- ☐ **a.** were wasteful.
- ☐ **b.** used their resources well.
- ☐ **c.** cared little about their environment.

5. You can also conclude that the Plains Indians probably believed that
- ☐ **a.** only the strongest creatures survive.
- ☐ **b.** each person must take care of himself or herself.
- ☐ **c.** if the balance of nature is upset, all creatures suffer.

C. Reading Strategies

1. Recognizing Words in Context

Find the word *respected* in the article. One definition below is closest to the meaning of that word. One definition has the opposite or nearly the opposite meaning. The remaining definition has a meaning that has nothing to do with the word. Label the definitions **C** for *closest,* **O** for *opposite* or *nearly opposite,* and **U** for *unrelated.*

_____ **a.** did not like

_____ **b.** made pictures of

_____ **c.** valued and admired

2. Distinguishing Fact from Opinion

Two of the statements below present *facts,* which can be proved. The other statement is an *opinion,* which expresses someone's thoughts or beliefs. Label the statements **F** for *fact* and **O** for *opinion.*

_____ **a.** The buffalo helped the Plains Indians survive.

_____ **b.** The Plains Indians used each part of the buffalo.

_____ **c.** Plains Indian men worked harder than the women did.

3. Making Correct Inferences

Two of the statements below are correct *inferences,* or reasonable guesses, that are based on information in the article. The other statement is an incorrect, or faulty, inference. Label the statements **C** for *correct* inference and **I** for *incorrect* inference.

_____ **a.** As buffalo herds moved, the Plains Indians moved with them.

_____ **b.** The Plains Indians took time to show thanks to the buffalo.

_____ **c.** The Plains Indians tried to kill each buffalo they saw.

4. Understanding Main Ideas

One of the statements below expresses the main idea of the article. Another statement is too general, or too broad. The other explains only part of the article; it is too narrow. Label the statements **M** for *main idea,* **B** for *too broad,* and **N** for *too narrow.*

_____ **a.** The Plains Indians respected buffalo and used them for food and other materials.

_____ **b.** The Plains Indians hunted many animals for food.

_____ **c.** Several groups of Plains Indians live in the Great Plains region.

5. Responding to the Article

Complete the following sentence in your own words:

What interested me most in "The Plains Indians and the Buffalo" was

____

____

D. Expanding Vocabulary

Content-Area Words

Read each item carefully. Write on the line the word or phrase that best completes each sentence.

1. People are most likely to hear sacred music in a ______________________.
   church shopping mall school
2. Grease may help ______________________ to function more smoothly.
   clothing car parts stairs
3. ______________________ is a vital human organ.
   A foot The heart The hair
4. Many schools have ceremonies when students ______________________.
   take tests graduate go on vacation
5. The role of a doctor is to ______________________.
   help sick people raise children direct movies

Academic English

In the article "The Plains Indians and the Buffalo," you learned that *prime* means "first in rank or importance." *Prime* can also mean "of the highest quality," as in the following sentence.

The cheese is expensive because it is of prime quality.

Complete the sentence below.

1. The *prime* seats in the theater are ____

Now use the word *prime* in a sentence of your own.

2. ____

   ____

You also learned that *assured* means "made certain." *Assured* can also mean "said with firm belief," as in the following sentence.

Tuan assured Matt that he would not forget to feed Matt's fish.

Complete the sentence below.

3. Our teacher *assured* us that the test ____

Now use the word *assured* in two sentences of your own.

4. ____
5. ____

Share your new sentences with a partner.

Vocabulary Assessment

Writing an Advertisement

Read the advertisement. Then complete the sentences. Use words from the Word Bank.

Use Gentle Gardener—Not Chemicals

Use Gentle Gardener to have a beautiful garden without harming the (1) ____________. Gentle Gardener (2) ____________ kills weeds, but it will not hurt flowers, fruits, or vegetables. It is just as (3) ____________ as weed killers that use strong chemicals. However, our product contains only natural ingredients. Be a careful (4) ____________—buy products that (5) ____________ safe air and soil.

Buy Gentle Gardener!

Word Bank

environment **promote**
efficiently **potent**
consumer

Reading an Award

Read the award. Circle the word that completes each sentence.

Award for Excellence in Medicine

Presented to Dr. Chea Lok
by Johnson City Hospital

Dr. Lok works with people who have (**contracted, revolted**) Parkinson's disease. People with this disease develop (**arrogant, rigid**) muscles, and it is hard for them to move. They (**guilty, desperately**) need a cure. Dr. Lok has done research on a medicine that (**defendants, functions**) to help muscles move more easily. Her research has become a (**vital, sacred**) part of the effort to find a cure for this disease.

Congratulations!

Making Connections

Work with a partner. Talk about what the words mean. How can you use the words to tell a story about a real or imaginary hero who helped people? List your ideas in the outline of the book below.

revolution	**publish**	**prime**	**assured**	**confined**
poverty	**role**	**legend**	**despite**	**present**

Use all of the words above in a paragraph of your own. Each sentence may include one or more of the words. To help you start writing, look at the ideas you wrote about. After you write your paragraph, read it over. If you find a mistake, correct it.

____

____

____

____

____

____

Everyday Life in the Middle Ages

Before You Read

Think about what you know. Skim the article on the opposite page. What do you predict the article will be about? What do you already know about Europe in the Middle Ages?

Vocabulary

The content-area and academic English words below appear in "Everyday Life in the Middle Ages." Read the definitions and the example sentences.

Content-Area Words

presented (pri zent′əd) produced

Example: The dead battery in the calculator *presented* a problem.

exchange (iks chānj′) to give an item or service in return for something of equal value

Example: I gave Tina a CD in *exchange* for her help with my homework.

tended (tend′əd) cared for; watched over

Example: Akemi *tended* her grandmother when she was sick.

starved (stärvd) died from hunger

Example: If Carlos had not fed the baby bird, it would have *starved.*

slaughtered (slô′tərd) killed an animal for food

Example: The farmer *slaughtered* a pig.

Academic English

consisted (kən sist′əd) was made up of

Example: The clown's outfit *consisted* of a curly green wig and giant shoes.

accompanied (ə kum′pə nēd) went with

Example: Dion's brother *accompanied* him to the basketball game.

Rate each vocabulary word according to the following scale. Write a number next to each content-area and academic English word.

4 I have never seen the word before.

3 I have seen the word but do not know what it means.

2 I know what the word means when I read it.

1 I use the word myself in speaking or writing.

Now skim the article and look for other words that are new to you. Write each new word and its definition in the Personal Dictionary.

While You Read

Tip! **Think about why you read.** Imagine that you are part of a peasant family in the Middle Ages. What do you do each day? As you read, look for answers to this question.

Everyday Life in the Middle Ages

The Middle Ages in Europe was a difficult time period. Everyday life was hard, and thieves and wild animals **presented** dangers. For protection, communities grew around central places called *manors*.

Manors **consisted** of a castle, a church, a village, and farmland. Every manor had a lord, who was in charge. Most of the people who lived on the manor were peasants. The manor system allowed the peasants to have land to farm, but the lord forced the peasants to pay high taxes. The peasants had to give him most of their crops. In **exchange** the lord protected the peasants from thieves and soldiers who passed through the manor. This protection was important in those dangerous times. This system of society was called *feudalism*. The lord was at the top of the system, and the peasants, or serfs, were at the bottom.

LANGUAGE CONNECTION

The phrase *in charge* means "in a position of power and authority." Lords were in charge of their manors. Who may be in charge of a classroom? A country? A family?

The lord expected a peasant man to spend up to 18 hours each day in the fields. A peasant woman spent her day around the house. She **tended** the garden and cared for the family livestock, or animals. She also spun thread for cloth, which she used to make clothing. She made candles from tallow, or animal fat, and she cooked all of the meals. Children also had to work. When a boy reached 10 years of age, he **accompanied** the men in the fields. Girls stayed with their mothers and learned to do chores. Peasants ate whatever they could grow, so it was very important for them to work hard. Their main crops were corn, beets, and wheat. Sometimes the weather was poor, and peasants lost their crops. Many people **starved** to death.

CONTENT CONNECTION

Look at the last two sentences of the third paragraph. Why did poor weather cause some peasants to starve? Explain the cause and effect in your own words.

Most peasant homes were cold and dark. They had dirt floors and thatched roofs made from plants. Peasants built walls from wood, stone, or mud-covered branches. If a home had windows, the windows were very small. This was because only wealthy people could afford to buy window glass. In the winter, peasants moved their livestock inside for warmth. Homes usually had only two rooms. The main room had a kitchen hearth, or fireplace. People used the hearth both to cook food and to heat the room. Peasants commonly ate breads, as well as vegetables from their gardens. They slept on stacks of straw. In the fall, they **slaughtered** their animals, and they used the meat for the whole year.

Many celebrations took place, however. People celebrated births and marriages, and they had feasts on religious holidays. Sometimes the lord of the manor provided food for the feast. At those times the people danced, and everyone had food.

After You Read

A. Organizing Ideas

How were the lives of peasants and lords similar and different? Complete the diagram below. In the left circle, list facts about peasants. In the right circle, list facts about lords. In the section where the two circles overlap, list facts that apply to both peasants and lords. Use the article to help you. Some have been done for you.

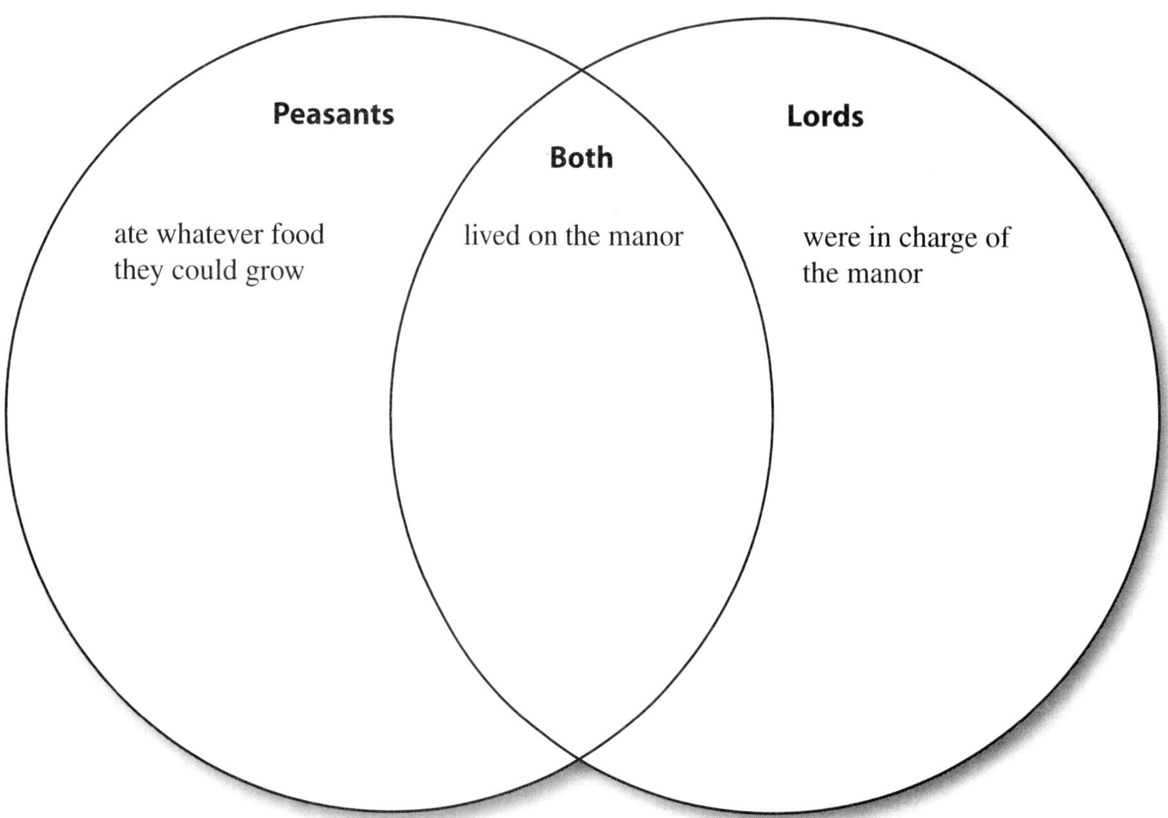

How did completing the diagram help you understand the manor system in the Middle Ages? Write two or more sentences to explain your answer. When could you use a diagram like this again?

B. Comprehension Skills

Tip! **Think about how to find answers.** Look back at what you read. The words in an answer are usually contained in a single sentence.

Mark box **a, b,** or **c** with an **X** before the choice that best completes each sentence.

Recalling Facts

1. Most people in the Middle Ages were
- ☐ **a.** lords.
- ☐ **b.** thieves.
- ☐ **c.** peasants.

2. A peasant man spent most of his time
- ☐ **a.** indoors.
- ☐ **b.** in the fields.
- ☐ **c.** hunting for food.

3. Manors included a castle, a church, a village, and
- ☐ **a.** a harbor.
- ☐ **b.** farmland.
- ☐ **c.** a railroad station.

4. The social system of the Middle Ages was
- ☐ **a.** feudalism.
- ☐ **b.** a proprietary system.
- ☐ **c.** an educational system.

5. Peasant homes had floors of
- ☐ **a.** dirt.
- ☐ **b.** wood.
- ☐ **c.** stone.

Understanding Ideas

1. From the article, you can conclude that feudalism was most helpful to
- ☐ **a.** lords.
- ☐ **b.** thieves.
- ☐ **c.** peasants.

2. It was most likely that a peasant farmer
- ☐ **a.** would one day be a lord.
- ☐ **b.** would always be a peasant farmer.
- ☐ **c.** would one day be able to start his own farm.

3. A person born in the Middle Ages was most likely to be a
- ☐ **a.** lord.
- ☐ **b.** priest.
- ☐ **c.** peasant.

4. Life for most people in the Middle Ages
- ☐ **a.** was very relaxing.
- ☐ **b.** involved a great deal of work.
- ☐ **c.** revolved around good education.

5. The main idea of the article is that
- ☐ **a.** manor life in the Middle Ages was hard for most people.
- ☐ **b.** a lord in the Middle Ages was in charge of a manor.
- ☐ **c.** people in the Middle Ages had wedding celebrations.

C. Reading Strategies

1. Recognizing Words in Context

Find the word *expected* in the article. One definition below is closest to the meaning of that word. One definition has the opposite or nearly the opposite meaning. The remaining definition has a meaning that has nothing to do with the word. Label the definitions **C** for *closest,* **O** for *opposite* or *nearly opposite,* and **U** for *unrelated.*

_____ **a.** did not allow
_____ **b.** required
_____ **c.** taught

2. Distinguishing Fact from Opinion

Two of the statements below present *facts,* which can be proved. The other statement is an *opinion,* which expresses someone's thoughts or beliefs. Label the statements **F** for *fact* and **O** for *opinion.*

_____ **a.** Lords treated the peasants fairly.
_____ **b.** Peasants depended on lords for protection.
_____ **c.** People in the Middle Ages celebrated religious holidays.

3. Making Correct Inferences

Two of the statements below are correct *inferences,* or reasonable guesses, that are based on information in the article. The other statement is an incorrect, or faulty, inference. Label the statements **C** for *correct* inference and **I** for *incorrect* inference.

_____ **a.** Peasants had little control over their daily lives.
_____ **b.** Lords could decide the amount of taxes to collect from peasants.
_____ **c.** Peasants did not like their lords.

4. Understanding Main Ideas

One of the statements below expresses the main idea of the article. Another statement is too general, or too broad. The other explains only part of the article; it is too narrow. Label the statements **M** for *main idea,* **B** for *too broad,* and **N** for *too narrow.*

_____ **a.** Life was hard during the Middle Ages.
_____ **b.** Peasants often starved when they did not have enough to eat.
_____ **c.** In the Middle Ages, peasants on manors worked hard in exchange for a lord's protection.

5. Responding to the Article

Complete the following sentence in your own words:
One thing in "Everyday Life in the Middle Ages" that I cannot understand is

____

____

D. Expanding Vocabulary

Content-Area Words

Complete each sentence with a word from the box. Write the missing word on the line.

presented	exchange	tended	starved	slaughtered

1. Nahee ________________ the store while the owner was on vacation.
2. When Tony gave me his phone number, I gave him mine in ________________.
3. The fallen tree ________________ a problem because it blocked the street.
4. Some of the people ________________ after diseases destroyed their crops.
5. Every year he ________________ a turkey for his Thanksgiving dinner.

Academic English

In the article "Everyday Life in the Middle Ages," you learned that *consisted* means "was made up of." *Consisted* can also mean "existed in," as in the following sentence.

For medieval peasants, safety consisted in working for a lord.

Complete the sentence below.

1. When I was a baby, happiness *consisted* in ________________________________

Now use the word *consisted* in a sentence of your own.

2. ____

____

You also learned that *accompanied* means "went with." *Accompanied* can also mean "existed or occurred in combination with," as in the following sentence.

Music accompanied the dance performance.

Complete the sentence below.

3. A celebration *accompanied* ________________________________

Now use the word *accompanied* in two sentences of your own.

4. ____
5. ____

Share your new sentences with a partner.

Lesson 17

The Euro: Coin of the European Union

Before You Read

Think about what you know. Read the lesson title above. Think about the words *euro* and *coin*. Then say the title in your own words. What are the names of coins and money that you have used?

Vocabulary

The content-area and academic English words below appear in "The Euro: Coin of the European Union." Read the definitions and the example sentences.

Content-Area Words

union (ūn′yən) a group that joins together for a common purpose
Example: The farmworkers formed a *union* to fight for better pay.

compete (kəm pēt′) to work against others to win a contest or prize
Example: Soccer teams from many countries *compete* for the World Cup.

treaty (trē′tē) an agreement signed by two or more countries or other groups
Example: The two countries signed a *treaty* to end their war.

resembles (ri zem′bəlz) looks like; is similar to
Example: Katrina *resembles* her mother in that they both have red hair.

emblem (em′bləm) an object or picture that represents another object or an idea
Example: The Statue of Liberty is an *emblem* of freedom.

Academic English

legal (lē′gəl) established or allowed by law
Example: It is not *legal* to drive over 25 miles per hour on the street in front of the school.

currency (kur′ən sē) money that people currently use
Example: The penny is one form of *currency* in the United States.

Read again the example sentences that follow the content-area and academic English word definitions. With a partner, discuss the meanings of the words and sentences. Then make up a sentence of your own for each word. Your teacher may wish to discuss your new sentences in class.

Now skim the article and look for other words that are new to you. Write each new word and its definition in the Personal Dictionary.

While You Read

Tip! **Think about why you read.** Do all euro coins look the same? Write down your guess to the answer of this question. As you read, look for the answer.

The Euro Coin of the European Union

The countries in the European **Union** (EU) have not always been friends. In the past, they often fought wars against each other. At the end of the most recent war, in 1945, some people decided that it was time for a change. They thought that it would be better to work together than to **compete.** The EU began in 1950 as a federation, or a group of officially joined nations. At that time, it had 6 members. Today it has 25.

Nations who wanted to build the union did not have an easy task. Each nation had to prove to its citizens that the union was a good idea. Finally, in 1993, the first 12 countries signed a formal **treaty.** This treaty created the EU. Since then the nations have worked together as a union. They have improved trade and increased their wealth. They also cooperate on issues such as laws and foreign relations. In 1998 EU members agreed to create a single form of money to be their **legal currency.**

Most EU countries use a form of money called the *euro*. People began to use it on the first day of 2002. The sign for the euro (€) **resembles** a capital *E*. One euro equals 100 euro cents. The euro system includes eight different coins and seven paper banknotes. The coins range from 1 cent up to 2 euros. The banknotes are worth from 5 to 500 euros.

The euro coin is an **emblem** of the union of different cultures. A map of Europe appears on one side of the coin, along with stars that stand for the member countries. Each nation chooses a special design for the other side of the coin. For example, every Netherlands coin has a picture of the queen of the Netherlands on it. Italy coins show some famous works of Italian art. All of the banknotes are the same. People can use any coin in any country that has switched to the new euro.

Most of the nations in the EU use the euro. Denmark, Sweden, and the United Kingdom still use their own money. However, these three countries may use the euro someday.

The new system is helpful for companies that do business in more than one country in the EU. It is also helpful for people who travel. For example, a person who plans to visit Paris, Athens, and Madrid no longer has to learn about French *francs,* Greek *drachmas,* and Spanish *pesetas.*

LANGUAGE CONNECTION

Look at the first sentence of the article. The word *friend* usually refers to a person. In your own words, tell what it means for two nations to be friends.

CONTENT CONNECTION

Before many European countries switched to the euro, people had to change currency when they traveled between the different countries. What problems would occur if every state in the United States suddenly started to use its own currency?

After You Read

A. Organizing Ideas

What do you know about the EU and its currency? Complete the outline below. On the lines, write down details that support the statements about the EU and the euro. Refer to the article to find information. Some have been done for you.

The European Union and the Euro

I. The European Union brought countries together.

A. Six nations formed a federation in 1950.

B. ______________________

C. ______________________

II. Most EU members use a common form of currency.

A. The euro is the currency that most EU nations use.

B. ______________________

C. ______________________

III. The euro has been helpful in many ways.

A. People can use euros in any member country that uses this currency.

B. ______________________

C. ______________________

Imagine that you must explain the euro system to someone who does not know about it. Write two or more sentences that you would use to describe the system to that person. How did this outline help you decide what to write?

____

____

____

____

____

____

B. Comprehension Skills

Tip! **Think about how to find answers.** Look back at different parts of the text. What facts help you figure out how to complete the sentences?

Mark box **a, b,** or **c** with an **X** before the choice that best completes each sentence.

Recalling Facts

1. The euro is the form of money that people
- ☐ **a.** once used in Europe.
- ☐ **b.** use in most of the EU countries.
- ☐ **c.** have used in Europe since 1950.

2. Each euro coin
- ☐ **a.** is worth 1 euro cent.
- ☐ **b.** can be used in only one country.
- ☐ **c.** has a map of Europe on one side.

3. The euro system is helpful for
- ☐ **a.** people who do not travel.
- ☐ **b.** countries that do business outside Europe.
- ☐ **c.** companies that do business in more than one EU country.

4. Two of the countries that use the euro are
- ☐ **a.** Denmark and Sweden.
- ☐ **b.** Italy and the Netherlands.
- ☐ **c.** the United Kingdom and Spain.

5. As nations worked to create the European Union, they faced the problem that
- ☐ **a.** nobody was interested.
- ☐ **b.** most countries already used the euro.
- ☐ **c.** countries that once were enemies would have to work together.

Understanding Ideas

1. Legal currency
- ☐ **a.** is almost worthless.
- ☐ **b.** is the official money of a country.
- ☐ **c.** must be changed into real money before people can use it.

2. It took a long time to agree on a single currency probably because
- ☐ **a.** each country thought that its money was a special part of the country.
- ☐ **b.** the countries of the EU did not often trade with each other.
- ☐ **c.** most nations refused to work together.

3. EU nations that once were enemies had to
- ☐ **a.** build trust over time.
- ☐ **b.** agree to speak one language.
- ☐ **c.** choose a common form of government.

4. EU members would probably agree that
- ☐ **a.** the switch to a single currency did not affect trade.
- ☐ **b.** shared success is better than the risk of failure alone.
- ☐ **c.** competition among members will result in a stronger EU.

5. The main reason that nations wanted to form the European Union was probably
- ☐ **a.** religious, or related to beliefs.
- ☐ **b.** cultural, or related to activities.
- ☐ **c.** economic, or related to money.

C. Reading Strategies

1. Recognizing Words in Context

Find the word *cooperate* in the article. One definition below is closest to the meaning of that word. One definition has the opposite or nearly the opposite meaning. The remaining definition has a meaning that has nothing to do with the word. Label the definitions **C** for *closest,* **O** for *opposite* or *nearly opposite,* and **U** for *unrelated.*

_____ **a.** work hard
_____ **b.** work against each other
_____ **c.** work together

2. Distinguishing Fact from Opinion

Two of the statements below present *facts,* which can be proved. The other statement is an *opinion,* which expresses someone's thoughts or beliefs. Label the statements **F** for *fact* and **O** for *opinion.*

_____ **a.** Some EU nations were enemies in the past.
_____ **b.** The EU officially began in 1993.
_____ **c.** All nations in the EU should use the euro.

3. Making Correct Inferences

Two of the statements below are correct *inferences,* or reasonable guesses, that are based on information in the article. The other statement is an incorrect, or faulty, inference. Label the statements **C** for *correct* inference and **I** for *incorrect* inference.

_____ **a.** People can spend euros in Sweden.
_____ **b.** The highest euro coin is worth 200 euro cents.
_____ **c.** More nations may join the EU in the future.

4. Understanding Main Ideas

One of the statements below expresses the main idea of the article. Another statement is too general, or too broad. The other explains only part of the article; it is too narrow. Label the statements **M** for *main idea,* **B** for *too broad,* and **N** for *too narrow.*

_____ **a.** Most nations in the EU use the same currency.
_____ **b.** The EU has brought nations together and created a common currency: the euro.
_____ **c.** The euro system is helpful for people who travel or do business in EU nations.

5. Responding to the Article

Complete the following sentence in your own words:
Before reading "The Euro: Coin of the European Union," I already knew

____

____

D. Expanding Vocabulary

Content-Area Words

Cross out one word in each row that is not related to the word in dark type.

1. **union**	join	common	together	coin
2. **compete**	design	fight	win	contest
3. **treaty**	agreement	cooperate	symbol	groups
4. **resembles**	similar	allows	common	alike
5. **emblem**	symbol	idea	represent	example

Academic English

In the article "The Euro: Coin of the European Union," you learned that *legal* means "established or allowed by law." In the article, *legal* refers to the currency of the European Union. *Legal* can also mean "relating to law," as in the following sentence.

A legal dictionary contains definitions of words that relate to laws.

Complete the sentence below.

1. An example of a *legal* document is a passport or a ______________________________

Now use the word *legal* in a sentence of your own.

2. ____

____

You also learned that *currency* means "money that people currently use." *Currency* can also mean "the state of being up-to-date or current," as in the following sentence.

Ibrahim checked the currency of Maya's phone number in the telephone book.

Complete the sentence below.

3. I doubted the *currency* of the travel book because ______________________________

Now use the word *currency* in two sentences of your own.

4. ____

5. ____

Share your new sentences with a partner.

Lesson 18 Farms in the Ancient Middle East

Before You Read

Think about what you know. Read the first sentence of the second paragraph of the article on the opposite page. What do you already know about the ways that people farm?

Vocabulary

The content-area and academic English words below appear in "Farms in the Ancient Middle East." Read the definitions and the example sentences.

Content-Area Words

extends (iks tendz′) continues in a certain direction for a certain distance
Example: The roof *extends* over the top of the house.

Fertile Crescent (furt′əl kres′ənt) a curved strip of land between the Mediterranean Sea and the Persian Gulf
Example: Ancient people settled in the *Fertile Crescent* because crops grew well there.

keen (kēn) sharp of mind; able to notice many details
Example: Eric had a *keen* mind for mathematics.

flourish (flur′ish) to grow or develop very successfully
Example: The children will *flourish* in their new school.

domesticate (də mes′tə kāt′) to change animals or plants from a wild state to a controlled state
Example: It may be difficult to *domesticate* a bear.

Academic English

implement (im′plə ment′) to begin to use something
Example: The town will *implement* the new law in June.

occurred (ə kurd′) took place
Example: The fire *occurred* because lightning struck a tree.

Do any of the words above seem related? Sort the seven vocabulary words into two or more categories. Write the words down on note cards or in a chart. Words may fit into more than one group. You may wish to work with a partner for this activity.

Now skim the article and look for other words that are new to you. Write each new word and its definition in the Personal Dictionary.

While You Read

Tip! **Think about why you read.** How did people live before they had farms? The main idea of the article is that farms helped change the way people live. As you read, try to find details that support the main idea.

Farms in the Ancient Middle East

People first began to farm thousands of years ago in the Middle East, which is part of Asia. The Middle East **extends** from the **Fertile Crescent** in the east to the Mediterranean Sea in the west. The Fertile Crescent is the arc of land between the Tigris (tī´gris) and Euphrates (ū frā´tēz) rivers. The Middle East is not just the first place where human beings grew crops. It is also the place where some of the world's first great cities and cultures existed. For some people, farms were just one of many ways to produce food. These people did not just hunt, and they did not just farm. They did both. For other people, farms became an important part of the culture.

How did people first learn to farm? No one knows for sure. Ancient people were involved in the natural world as much as the animals in the forests and the birds in the skies were. They made **keen** observations about the living things around them. They probably noticed that plants grew from seeds that fell on the ground. At first people gathered the plants where they grew in the wild. They began to **implement** farming when they collected seeds and planted them nearer to where they lived.

People first grew grain crops such as barley and wheat. They could dry these grains and store them for a long time. This gave them food to eat when hunting did not go well.

When fields produced food, people settled down and built homes. Because they had a steady food supply, they lived longer and had more children. Larger numbers of people turned small villages into towns and cities. In other words, in some places farms came first and towns grew around them. In other areas, people built towns before they began to farm. In these places, people may have started to farm because they could no longer hunt for or gather enough food.

About 10,000 years ago, both farms and populations began to **flourish.** More food supported growing numbers of people. People could then produce even more food. During this time, called the *Neolithic Age* or the *New Stone Age,* people began to **domesticate** animals. Rather than hunt animals, people started to raise them for food. Some scholars call the changes that **occurred** because of farms the *Neolithic Revolution.* Within about 2,000 years, farmers in the Middle East began to grow more kinds of grain. They also began to grow vegetables such as lentils and peas.

CONTENT CONNECTION

When people first began to farm, the Middle East was a large area with no governments or countries. Today the Middle East contains many countries. What Middle Eastern countries do you know of?

LANGUAGE CONNECTION

In the fourth paragraph, the phrase *settled down* means "began to live in one place." *Settled down* can also mean "became less excited or nervous." Try to use the second definition of *settled down* in a sentence.

After You Read

A. Organizing Ideas

How did ancient people become farmers? Complete the chart below. In each circle, write a sentence to describe an event in the history of farming. List the events in order. Use information from the article. Some have been done for you.

How Ancient People Became Farmers

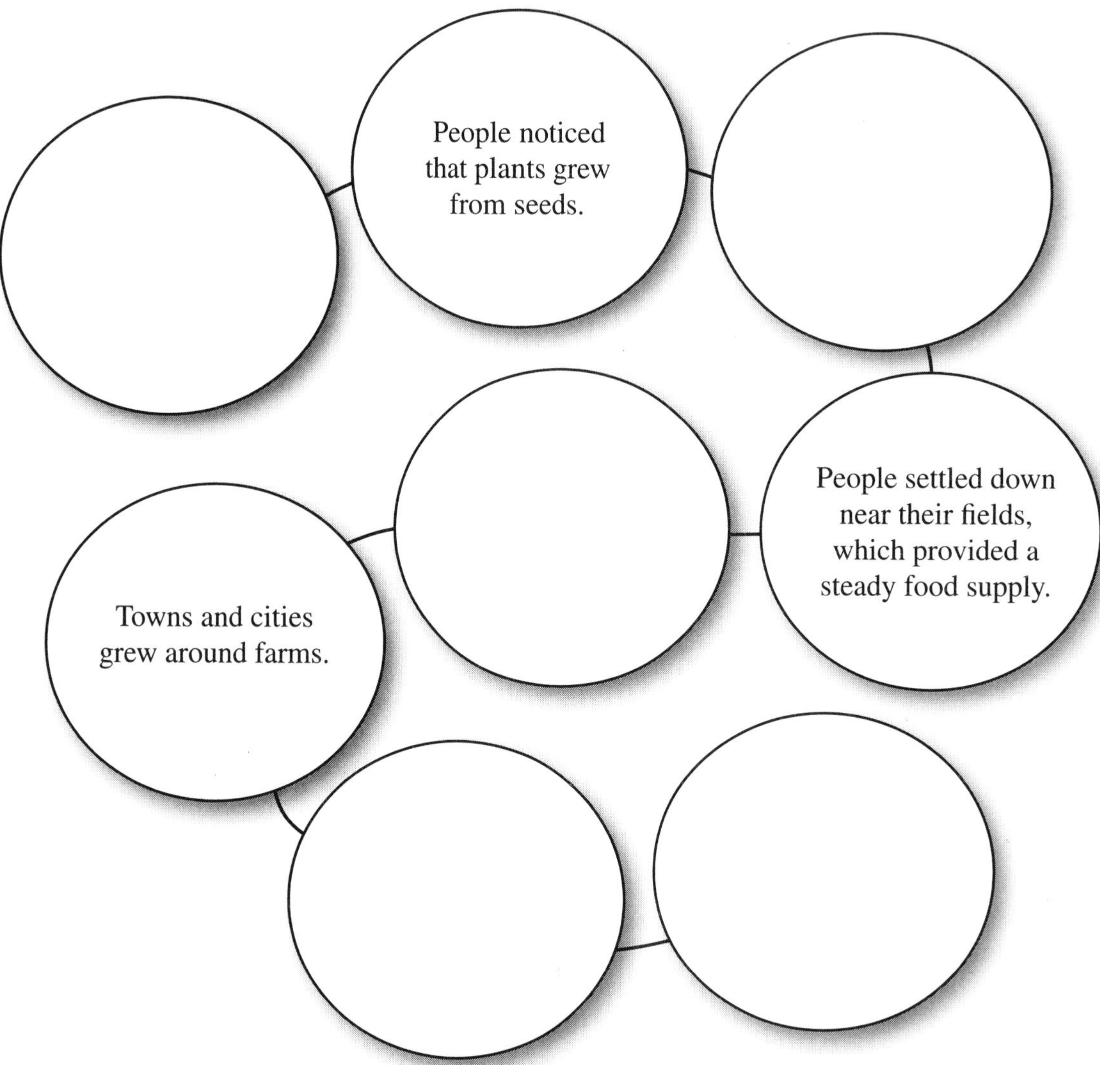

How did this chart help you understand how farming changed the way of life for ancient people? Write two or more sentences to explain your answer. How else could you organize the information in the chart?

B. Comprehension Skills

 **Think about how to find answers.** Think about what each sentence means. Try to say it to yourself in your own words before you complete it.

Mark box **a, b,** or **c** with an **X** before the choice that best completes each sentence.

Recalling Facts

1. People first began to farm thousands of years ago
- ☐ **a.** in Europe.
- ☐ **b.** in the Middle East.
- ☐ **c.** along the Rhine River.

2. The first crops that people grew were
- ☐ **a.** fruit trees.
- ☐ **b.** grains such as barley and wheat.
- ☐ **c.** vegetables such as lentils and peas.

3. A steady food supply allowed people to
- ☐ **a.** hunt more often.
- ☐ **b.** move from place to place.
- ☐ **c.** live longer and have more children.

4. Another name for the Neolithic Age is the
- ☐ **a.** New Stone Age.
- ☐ **b.** Fertile Crescent.
- ☐ **c.** Middle Ages.

5. The Fertile Crescent is located
- ☐ **a.** in Europe.
- ☐ **b.** next to the Mediterranean Sea.
- ☐ **c.** between the Tigris and Euphrates.

Understanding Ideas

1. Farming in the Middle East
- ☐ **a.** is a modern discovery.
- ☐ **b.** began before towns appeared.
- ☐ **c.** completely replaced hunting during the Neolithic Age.

2. New ways to get food
- ☐ **a.** led to changes to the way of life.
- ☐ **b.** had little impact on people.
- ☐ **c.** caused people to grow too much food during the Neolithic Age.

3. Farming became an important part of human culture
- ☐ **a.** at different times for different groups.
- ☐ **b.** at about the same time that people learned to hunt.
- ☐ **c.** only after hunting and gathering no longer supplied enough food.

4. To say that farms and populations began to flourish means that
- ☐ **a.** life became a great struggle.
- ☐ **b.** most people moved to cities.
- ☐ **c.** the number of farms and people grew.

5. The Neolithic Revolution refers to
- ☐ **a.** a war between Neolithic groups.
- ☐ **b.** the growth of farms and towns during a certain time.
- ☐ **c.** the discovery that metal tools worked well for farming.

C. Reading Strategies

1. Recognizing Words in Context

Find the word *observations* in the article. One definition below is closest to the meaning of that word. One definition has the opposite or nearly the opposite meaning. The remaining definition has a meaning that has nothing to do with the word. Label the definitions **C** for *closest,* **O** for *opposite* or *nearly opposite,* and **U** for *unrelated.*

_____ **a.** things that people notice
_____ **b.** things that people want
_____ **c.** things that people ignore

2. Distinguishing Fact from Opinion

Two of the statements below present *facts,* which can be proved. The other statement is an *opinion,* which expresses someone's thoughts or beliefs. Label the statements **F** for *fact* and **O** for *opinion.*

_____ **a.** No one knows for sure how people first learned to farm.
_____ **b.** People grew crops before they raised animals for food.
_____ **c.** Life on a farm is more pleasant than life in a city.

3. Making Correct Inferences

Two of the statements below are correct *inferences,* or reasonable guesses, that are based on information in the article. The other statement is an incorrect, or faulty, inference. Label the statements **C** for *correct* inference and **I** for *incorrect* inference.

_____ **a.** Hunters and gatherers had to move to different places to find food.
_____ **b.** When people began to farm, they no longer hunted for or gathered food.
_____ **c.** Farmers had a steadier food supply than hunters or gatherers did.

4. Understanding Main Ideas

One of the statements below expresses the main idea of the article. Another statement is too general, or too broad. The other explains only part of the article; it is too narrow. Label the statements **M** for *main idea,* **B** for *too broad,* and **N** for *too narrow.*

_____ **a.** Farms allowed ancient people to settle down and form towns.
_____ **b.** The first farmers grew grain crops in the Middle East.
_____ **c.** People have been farming for thousands of years.

5. Responding to the Article

Complete the following sentences in your own words:

One of the things I did best while reading "Farms in the Ancient Middle East" was

____

I think that I did this well because ___________________________________

____

D. Expanding Vocabulary

Content-Area Words

Read each item carefully. Write on the line the word or phrase that best completes each sentence.

1. People began to domesticate ________________ long ago.
   dogs sharks grass
2. A person should read books to help his or her ________________ flourish.
   mind library eyes
3. The beach extends ________________ in both directions.
   for several miles into the house onto the highway
4. The first ________________ probably appeared in the Fertile Crescent.
   cities rivers trees
5. Dogs with an exceptionally keen ________________ can help search for lost people.
   sense of sight sense of smell love of strangers

Academic English

In the article "Farms in the Ancient Middle East," you learned that *implement* is a verb that means "to begin to use something." *Implement* can also be a noun that means "a tool," as in the following sentence.

We need a sharp implement, such as a pair of scissors, to open the package.

Complete the sentence below.

1. One important *implement* for a gardener is ________________________________

Now use the word *implement* in a sentence of your own.

2. ____

____

You also learned that *occurred* means "took place." *Occurred* can also mean "came to mind," as in the following sentence.

It never occurred to Bonita that the store might be closed when she got there.

Complete the sentence below.

3. It *occurred* to the doctor that ________________________________

Now use the word *occurred* in two sentences of your own.

4. ____
5. ____

Share your new sentences with a partner.

Lesson 19

Renaissance Sports and Games

Before You Read

Think about what you know. Read the title and the first paragraph of the article on the opposite page. Which of those sports have you watched or played? What sports do you like to play?

Vocabulary

The content-area and academic English words below appear in "Renaissance Sports and Games." Read the definitions and the example sentences.

Content-Area Words

pastime (pas′tīm′) an activity that helps people pass time in a pleasant way
Example: My favorite *pastime* is reading books.

obstacles (ob′stə kəlz) things that stand in the way or make something more difficult
Example: Pilar had to climb large rocks and other *obstacles* on her hike.

strokes (strōks) movements, such as hits, that people do with tools
Example: I hammered the nail into the wood with steady *strokes*.

opponents (ə pō′nənts) people who work against each other, such as in a game
Example: Frank beat all of his *opponents* in the chess tournament.

boundaries (boun′dər ēz) objects or lines that show limits
Example: A fence marks the *boundaries* of my backyard.

Academic English

objective (əb jek′tiv) a goal or result that someone works toward
Example: The *objective* of some card games is for the players to get rid of all of their cards.

target (tär′git) an object or a mark to aim for
Example: Natalya hit the center of the paper *target* with her arrow.

Answer the questions below. Circle the part of each question that is the answer. The first one has been done for you.

1. Is (a card game) or a visit to the dentist more likely to be a favorite *pastime?*
2. Which has clear *boundaries*, the sky or a park?
3. Would it be easier to hit a large or small *target?*
4. Do basketball *opponents* pass the ball to or take the ball from each other?
5. Do *obstacles* make a task easier or harder?
6. Is the *objective* of soccer to score the least points or the most points?
7. Would a person use *strokes* to paint a wall or to do homework?

Now skim the article and look for other words that are new to you. Write each new word and its definition in the Personal Dictionary.

While You Read

Tip! **Think about why you read.** Have you ever invented a game? Do you know how your favorite sport began? As you read, decide which sport or game in the article has the most interesting history.

Many sports that people play today began or became popular in Europe during the Renaissance, in the fifteenth and sixteenth centuries. Some of these sports are golf, tennis, badminton, and bowls.

Golf began in Scotland. People believe that the ancient Scots played a game similar to golf. In this game, they hit pebbles, or small stones, into rabbit holes with sticks. By the 1400s, people called this **pastime** *golf*. The **objective** of golf is to hit a ball with sticks called *clubs* into a hole in the distance. Players use a huge, open area that contains **obstacles** such as sand traps, woods, and ponds. The player who gets the ball into the distant hole in the fewest **strokes** wins. Before the 1400s, Scots played golf anywhere and everywhere. A flying golf ball could injure citizens. Therefore people made a law that required golfers to play in areas set aside as golf courses.

Tennis also became popular during the Renaissance. Tennis **opponents** stand on opposite sides of a net. The net is in the middle of the tennis court. Lines on the floor of the court mark the **boundaries** of play. To play, one player hits the ball with a racket. The ball must go over the net to the opponent's side. The other player must hit the ball back over the net. If a player hits the ball out of bounds or lets the ball bounce more than once, the opponent wins the point. Early tennis players hit the ball with their hands instead of with rackets.

Badminton also began during the Renaissance. This game is related to tennis. To play badminton, opponents hit a lightweight, cone-shaped shuttlecock over a net with their rackets. People also call shuttlecocks *birdies*. Historians believe that shuttlecocks developed because people stuck bird feathers into corks. During the Renaissance, people dipped feathers in ink and wrote with them. They stored the feathers in corks.

Perhaps the most common Renaissance game was bowls. People could play bowls anywhere outdoors. Players drew a boundary circle on the ground. Then one player threw a small **target,** a ball called a *jack,* into the circle. Each player had four larger balls, called *bowls*. One by one, players tossed the bowls into the circle. The player who tossed a bowl closest to the jack won the game. Bowls is still popular today, especially in Italy. In Italy people call the game *bocce*.

CONTENT CONNECTION

Today golf is a popular sport in the United States. Male professional golf players compete in four major competitions each year. One of these competitions is the PGA Championship. What famous golfers do you know of?

LANGUAGE CONNECTION

Cone-shaped means "shaped like a cone" or "in the shape of a cone." An ice cream cone is cone-shaped. What other objects are cone-shaped?

After You Read

A. Organizing Ideas

What have you learned about Renaissance sports and games? Complete the chart below. In the columns, write down facts to explain the equipment, playing area, and objective of each game. Use information from the article. Some have been done for you.

Game	Equipment	Playing Area	Objective
golf			Players try to get the ball into the holes with the fewest strokes.
tennis	a net, a ball, rackets		
		a playing area with two sides that are divided by a net	Players hit the shuttlecock back and forth over the net and score points if an opponent lets it hit the ground or hits it out of bounds.
	one small target ball, four larger balls per player	a circle-shaped area on the ground	

How did completing this chart help you compare the games in the article? Which game would you most enjoy? Write two or more sentences to explain your answer. How could you use a chart like this again?

B. Comprehension Skills

 **Think about how to find answers.** Look back at what you read. The information is in the text, but you may have to look in several sentences to find it.

Mark box **a, b,** or **c** with an **X** before the choice that best completes each sentence.

Recalling Facts

1. People first played golf
- ☐ **a.** in Scotland.
- ☐ **b.** in the woods.
- ☐ **c.** in ancient Rome.

2. People often need several strokes to get a golf ball into the hole because
- ☐ **a.** the hole is far away.
- ☐ **b.** the ball is very small.
- ☐ **c.** they use weak sticks to hit the ball.

3. In early tennis, people hit balls with
- ☐ **a.** rackets.
- ☐ **b.** long sticks.
- ☐ **c.** their hands.

4. The shuttlecock developed from
- ☐ **a.** the lightweight tennis ball.
- ☐ **b.** goose feathers that people boiled.
- ☐ **c.** feathers that people stored in corks.

5. In bowls a player wins if his or her bowl
- ☐ **a.** is closest to the jack.
- ☐ **b.** becomes the target jack.
- ☐ **c.** knocks the jack out of the circle.

Understanding Ideas

1. Badminton is like tennis because
- ☐ **a.** the players hit shuttlecocks.
- ☐ **b.** the players hit an object over a net.
- ☐ **c.** the object that players hit is not allowed to touch the ground.

2. From the article, you can conclude that
- ☐ **a.** most badminton players also play tennis.
- ☐ **b.** tennis probably existed before badminton.
- ☐ **c.** badminton players are usually good at bowls.

3. You can also conclude that
- ☐ **a.** golfers should avoid the obstacles.
- ☐ **b.** no one played golf before the 1400s.
- ☐ **c.** pebbles replaced golf balls during the 1400s.

4. During the Renaissance,
- ☐ **a.** people had no time to play games.
- ☐ **b.** competition was discouraged.
- ☐ **c.** games were a popular pastime.

5. Bowls was probably the most common Renaissance game because
- ☐ **a.** it was invented in Italy.
- ☐ **b.** people could play it anywhere.
- ☐ **c.** players did not have to use rackets.

C. Reading Strategies

1. Recognizing Words in Context

Find the word *related* in the article. One definition below is closest to the meaning of that word. One definition has the opposite or nearly the opposite meaning. The remaining definition has a meaning that has nothing to do with the word. Label the definitions **C** for *closest,* **O** for *opposite* or *nearly opposite,* and **U** for *unrelated.*

_____ **a.** connected to
_____ **b.** very different from
_____ **c.** harder than

2. Distinguishing Fact from Opinion

Two of the statements below present *facts,* which can be proved. The other statement is an *opinion,* which expresses someone's thoughts or beliefs. Label the statements **F** for *fact* and **O** for *opinion.*

_____ **a.** Obstacles make golf less fun to play.
_____ **b.** A shuttlecock is part of the equipment for badminton.
_____ **c.** Today people in Italy use the word *bocce* for the game of bowls.

3. Making Correct Inferences

Two of the statements below are correct *inferences,* or reasonable guesses, that are based on information in the article. The other statement is an incorrect, or faulty, inference. Label the statements **C** for *correct* inference and **I** for *incorrect* inference.

_____ **a.** In golf the player with the highest score loses.
_____ **b.** Tennis players try to hit the ball before it bounces twice.
_____ **c.** People must understand tennis rules before they can play badminton.

4. Understanding Main Ideas

One of the statements below expresses the main idea of the article. Another statement is too general, or too broad. The other explains only part of the article; it is too narrow. Label the statements **M** for *main idea,* **B** for *too broad,* and **N** for *too narrow.*

_____ **a.** People have enjoyed different sports and games throughout history.
_____ **b.** Badminton and tennis are two related Renaissance sports.
_____ **c.** Many popular sports and games began during the Renaissance.

5. Responding to the Article

Complete the following sentence in your own words:
Reading "Renaissance Sports and Games" made me want to learn more about

____

because ____

____

D. Expanding Vocabulary

Content-Area Words

Complete each sentence with a word from the box. Write the missing word on the line.

pastime	obstacles	strokes	opponents	boundaries

1. Guards often check passports when people cross the ________________ of a country.
2. In Mei's family, the game of mah jongg is a popular ________________.
3. My parents faced many ________________ in their efforts to buy a new home.
4. After a friendly game of baseball, my team ate pizza with our ________________.
5. The man used steady ax ________________ as he chopped firewood.

Academic English

In the article "Renaissance Sports and Games," you learned that *objective* is a noun that means "a goal or result that someone works toward." *Objective* can also be an adjective that means "fair" or "able to consider the facts without personal feelings," as in the following sentence.

If Marco entered a talent competition, his mother would not be an objective judge.

Complete the sentence below.

1. Delia finds it hard to be *objective* when ________________________________

Now use the word *objective* in a sentence of your own.

2. ____

____

You also learned that *target* means "an object or a mark to aim for." *Target* can also mean "a goal to achieve," as in the following sentence.

The target of Ms. Prasad's class was to read 300 books in one year.

Complete the sentence below.

3. The *target* of our bake sale is to raise ________________________________

Now use the word *target* in two sentences of your own.

4. ____
5. ____

Share your new sentences with a partner.

Lesson 20

Early Days of the Grand Canal

Before You Read

Think about what you know. Skim the article on the opposite page. What do you predict the article will be about? Do you live near any waterways, such as rivers or canals? Have you ever heard of the Grand Canal?

Vocabulary

The content-area and academic English words below appear in "Early Days of the Grand Canal." Read the definitions and the example sentences.

Content-Area Words

engineers (en´ji nērz′) people trained to design, build, or use machines or structures
Example: The *engineers* designed the bridge over the river.

cargo (kär′gō) goods carried by a ship, plane, or other vehicle
Example: The *cargo* on the plane included medical supplies for the soldiers.

damaged (dam′ijd) hurt; made less valuable or useful
Example: Ron accidentally *damaged* the book when he spilled water on it.

barges (bär′jəz) boats that have flat bottoms and that transport goods
Example: The *barges* carried cars across the lake.

banks (bangks) areas of land that rise along the edges of a body of water
Example: Trees and flowers grew along the *banks* of the river.

Academic English

significant (sig nif′i kənt) large in amount or quantity
Example: It will take a *significant* amount of time to knit a blanket.

abandoned (ə ban′dənd) gave something up completely
Example: Maria *abandoned* her bike when the chain fell off of it.

Complete the sentences below that contain the content-area and academic English words above. Use the spaces provided. The first one has been done for you.

1. Car *engineers* try to improve the way a car runs.
2. I *abandoned* my plans to have a picnic because ______.
3. A person may see *barges* on ______.
4. The *cargo* in the trunk of a family car may include ______.
5. Shruti spent a *significant* amount of time on ______.
6. The grassy, shady *banks* of the river are a good place to ______.
7. After he *damaged* the cup, it ______.

Now skim the article and look for other words that are new to you. Write each new word and its definition in the Personal Dictionary.

While You Read

Tip! Think about why you read. When did the people of China decide to build the first Grand Canal? Why did they build it? As you read, look for the answers to these questions.

Early Days of the Grand Canal

China is a very big country. It is slightly bigger than the United States in land area. China has many resources, including many great rivers. The rivers provide useful routes to transport, or move, goods. Water transport is a fast and easy way to carry heavy loads, such as large amounts of grain.

In ancient times, people needed a waterway to connect China's rich farmlands to the capital city. To fill this need, **engineers** built a waterway called a *canal*. The ancient thinker Confucius wrote that people began to work on a canal in about 486 B.C. This canal linked the Yangtze (yäng´tse´) River with the city of Huai-yin. Then for many centuries Chinese emperors had crews work to extend, or lengthen, this ancient canal.

Today the Chinese call this canal the *Da Yun He*. Its English name is "China's Grand Canal." One thousand years after workers built the original canal, it needed **significant** repairs. This was in A.D. 607, during the Sui dynasty. By 610 the emperor and his workers had extended the canal. The Grand Canal formed a northeast–southwest link between Huang Ho in the north and the Huai River in the south. The canal remained the main waterway in this part of China for the next 500 years.

By the thirteenth century, the Mongols had taken over China. The Yuan dynasty made Beijing the capital. The city's growing population needed more food, so workers built a new canal to link Beijing to the Grand Canal. This part of the Grand Canal took great effort and cost to complete. Builders tried twice without success, so they chose another route. Finally they finished this link in the Grand Canal. However, merchants found that it cost too much to use it. Instead they shipped food to Beijing by sea.

By the Ming dynasty (1368–1644), the Grand Canal had six sections. These sections were busy with **cargo** until the nineteenth century. Then a series of severe floods struck China. Floodwaters badly **damaged** parts of the Grand Canal. By 1868 the Chinese had mostly **abandoned** it for water transport. After a while it was in very bad condition—especially along its northern route.

Workers mostly restored the Grand Canal in the twentieth century. They widened and deepened it. They also constructed a new section. Today the canal, which is about 1,200 miles long, has new locks. The locks raise or lower water levels to help ships move through the canal. Many ships and **barges** use the canal. They carry goods to and from the cities along its **banks.**

LANGUAGE CONNECTION

The word *transport* appears twice in the first paragraph. Which time does it act as a verb? Which time does it act as a noun? How can you tell?

CONTENT CONNECTION

Why do you think the builders could not finish the canal to Beijing the first two times they tried? Hint: Think about why they may have had to find a new route.

After You Read

A. Organizing Ideas

What events shaped the history of the Grand Canal? Complete the chart below. In the first column, list important events in the history of the Grand Canal. In the second column, list the effects caused by each event. Refer to the article for information. Some have been done for you.

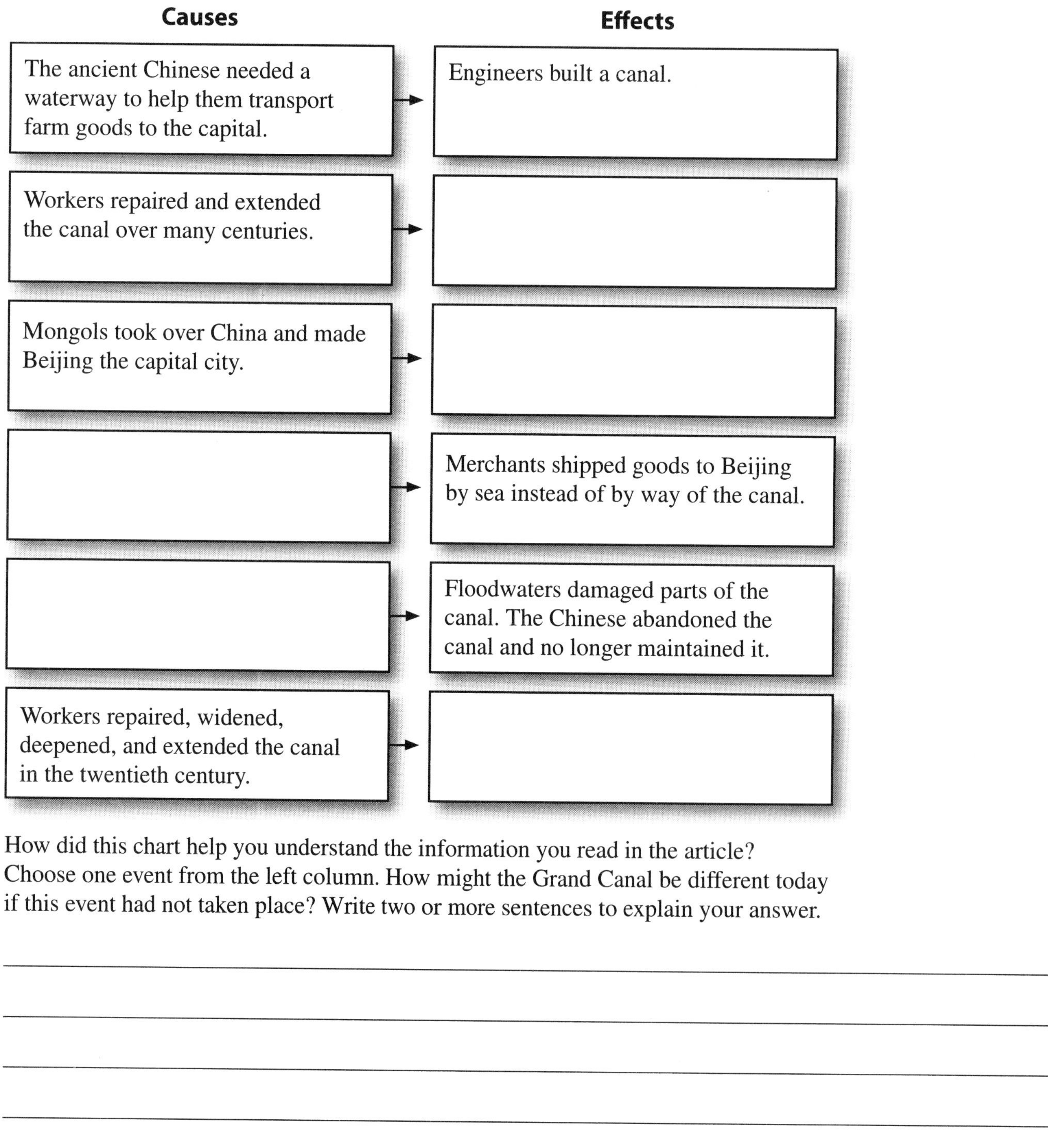

Causes	Effects
The ancient Chinese needed a waterway to help them transport farm goods to the capital.	Engineers built a canal.
Workers repaired and extended the canal over many centuries.	
Mongols took over China and made Beijing the capital city.	
	Merchants shipped goods to Beijing by sea instead of by way of the canal.
	Floodwaters damaged parts of the canal. The Chinese abandoned the canal and no longer maintained it.
Workers repaired, widened, deepened, and extended the canal in the twentieth century.	

How did this chart help you understand the information you read in the article? Choose one event from the left column. How might the Grand Canal be different today if this event had not taken place? Write two or more sentences to explain your answer.

B. Comprehension Skills

Tip! Think about how to find answers. Read each sentence below. Underline the words that will help you figure out how to complete each item.

Mark box **a, b,** or **c** with an **X** before the choice that best completes each sentence.

Recalling Facts

1. Confucius was a Chinese
- ☐ **a.** priest.
- ☐ **b.** thinker.
- ☐ **c.** merchant.

2. The first significant repairs to the canal took place around
- ☐ **a.** 486 B.C.
- ☐ **b.** A.D. 607.
- ☐ **c.** A.D. 1126.

3. The Grand Canal connects regions of China from
- ☐ **a.** east to west.
- ☐ **b.** north to west.
- ☐ **c.** northeast to southwest.

4. People built the Grand Canal to provide
- ☐ **a.** water for farmlands.
- ☐ **b.** easy transportation for the emperor's army.
- ☐ **c.** water transport between farmlands and the capital.

5. Today the Grand Canal is approximately
- ☐ **a.** 100 miles long.
- ☐ **b.** 750 miles long.
- ☐ **c.** 1,200 miles long.

Understanding Ideas

1. The Grand Canal was built to
- ☐ **a.** defend China from the Mongols.
- ☐ **b.** connect rivers to cities in China.
- ☐ **c.** improve food production in China.

2. In the thirteenth century, the cost to ship food on the Grand Canal was
- ☐ **a.** lower than the cost to ship by sea.
- ☐ **b.** higher than the cost to ship by sea.
- ☐ **c.** about the same as the cost to ship by sea.

3. From the article, you can conclude that a water transport system was a good idea for China because China has
- ☐ **a.** many rivers.
- ☐ **b.** many mountains.
- ☐ **c.** an extremely long coastline.

4. You can also conclude that the engineers who worked on the Grand Canal
- ☐ **a.** found solutions to their problems.
- ☐ **b.** worked with limited knowledge, skills, and money.
- ☐ **c.** earned a great deal of money for their achievement.

5. You can predict that in the future the Grand Canal will probably
- ☐ **a.** need some repairs.
- ☐ **b.** be extended to reach other countries.
- ☐ **c.** be abandoned when people begin to ship goods by plane.

C. Reading Strategies

1. Recognizing Words in Context

Find the word *restored* in the article. One definition below is closest to the meaning of that word. One definition has the opposite or nearly the opposite meaning. The remaining definition has a meaning that has nothing to do with the word. Label the definitions **C** for *closest,* **O** for *opposite* or *nearly opposite,* and **U** for *unrelated.*

_____ **a.** admired

_____ **b.** destroyed

_____ **c.** fixed

2. Distinguishing Fact from Opinion

Two of the statements below present *facts,* which can be proved. The other statement is an *opinion,* which expresses someone's thoughts or beliefs. Label the statements **F** for *fact* and **O** for *opinion.*

_____ **a.** People have added new sections to the Grand Canal over time.

_____ **b.** The Grand Canal is the most impressive structure built by ancient people.

_____ **c.** The Grand Canal is still used to ship goods today.

3. Making Correct Inferences

Two of the statements below are correct *inferences,* or reasonable guesses, that are based on information in the article. The other statement is an incorrect, or faulty, inference. Label the statements **C** for *correct* inference and **I** for *incorrect* inference.

_____ **a.** People built different parts of the Grand Canal at different times.

_____ **b.** Some sections of the Grand Canal are many years older than other sections.

_____ **c.** The Chinese did not ship goods on rivers before the Grand Canal was built.

4. Understanding Main Ideas

One of the statements below expresses the main idea of the article. Another statement is too general, or too broad. The other explains only part of the article; it is too narrow. Label the statements **M** for *main idea,* **B** for *too broad,* and **N** for *too narrow.*

_____ **a.** The Grand Canal is 1,200 miles long and runs northeast to southwest.

_____ **b.** The Grand Canal provides water transport for parts of China.

_____ **c.** The Grand Canal links regions of China and has been built and improved over many years.

5. Responding to the Article

Complete the following sentence in your own words:

One thing in "Early Days of the Grand Canal" that I cannot understand is

____

____

D. Expanding Vocabulary

Content-Area Words

Cross out one word or phrase in each row that is not related to the word in dark type.

1. **engineers**	populations	builds	designs	structures
2 **cargo**	goods	ship	plane	pencil
3. **damaged**	ruined	extended	hurt	less valuable
4. **barges**	boats	flat	land	transport
5. **banks**	shore	edges	water	grain

Academic English

In the article "Early Days of the Grand Canal," you learned that *significant* means "large in amount or quantity." *Significant* can also mean "important" or "meaningful," as in the following sentence.

High school graduation is a significant time for a student.

Complete the sentence below.

1. A *significant* event in my life was ______________________________

Now use the word *significant* in a sentence of your own.

2. ______________________________

____

You also learned that *abandoned* means "gave something up completely." *Abandoned* can also mean "gave in without trying not to," as in the following sentence.

The child abandoned herself to the joy of running through the field.

Complete the sentence below.

3. The audience *abandoned* itself to laughter when ______________________________

Now use the word *abandoned* in two sentences of your own.

4. ______________________________

5. ______________________________

Share your new sentences with a partner.

Writing a Postcard

Read the postcard. Then complete the sentences. Use words from the Word Bank.

Word Bank
- **currency**
- **occurred**
- **exchange**
- **flourish**
- **abandoned**

Hello, Josefa! Greetings from Goldfield, Nevada—an old mining town. It began to (1) ______________ when thousands of miners moved west to search for gold. In the early 1900s, miners found thousands of dollars worth of gold each day! They used gold as (2) ______________. They gave it to merchants in (3) ______________ for goods such as food and clothing. The miners (4) ______________ Goldfield after the gold ran out. A fire (5) ______________ in 1923 and destroyed part of the town. However, visitors can still see many old buildings and an old mine.

See you soon!—Mee

Josefa Garcia
2468 Your Street
Your Town, Your State
54321

Reading a Brochure

Read the brochure. Circle the word that completes each sentence.

Happy Trails Campground

At Happy Trails Campground, you'll camp along the (**banks, obstacles**) of the White River.

You can hike along a trail that (**resembles, extends**) for miles into a pine forest, or you can ride a canoe down the calm river. A Happy Trails staff member can give you even more ideas for activities. The (**objective, emblem**) of our staff is to make sure that you and your family have a wonderful vacation.

Past visitors have loved Happy Trails:

"My favorite (**pastime, cargo**) is bird-watching, and a Happy Trails staff member told me the best place to see rare bird species."

"Our family took a hike, and a Happy Trails tour guide (**damaged, accompanied**) us. She pointed out interesting trees and animals. We all learned a lot!"

No other campground can compete with Happy Trails!

Making Connections

Work with a partner. List the words in the first column. In the second column, briefly explain what each word means. In the third column, explain how you can use the word in writing or in a conversation.

legal	**consisted**	**implement**	**significant**	**target**
union	**boundaries**	**presented**	**domesticate**	**starved**

Word	What It Means	How I Can Use It

Use all of the words above in a paragraph of your own. Each sentence may include one or more of the words. To help you start writing, look at the ideas in the third column of the chart. After you write your paragraph, read it over. If you find a mistake, correct it.

____

____

____

____

____

____

____

Glossary

A

***abandoned** (ə ban′dənd) gave something up completely [20]

***accompanied** (ə kum′pə nēd) went with [16]

***adapted** (ə dapt′əd) changed in order to meet new needs [1]

archaeologist (är′kē ol′ə jist) a person who digs up and studies the remains of ancient cities to learn how people lived long ago [6]

architects (är′kə tekts′) people who design, draw plans for, or manage building projects [3]

arrogant (ar′ə gənt) too proud; believing oneself to be better than others [11]

artifacts (är′tə fakts′) objects made and used by ancient people [6]

association (ə sō′sē ā′shən) an organized group of people with common interests or purposes [7]

***assured** (ə shoord′) made certain [15]

astronauts (as′trə nôts′) people who fly or operate a spacecraft [8]

***automatic** (ô′tə mat′ik) done without extra thought or outside control [7]

B

ballads (bal′ədz) songs that tell stories in many short verses [1]

banks (bangks) areas of land that rise along the edges of a body of water [20]

barges (bär′jəz) boats that have flat bottoms and that transport goods [20]

boundaries (boun′dər ēz) objects or lines that show limits [19]

budget (buj′it) a plan for how to spend money on different things [14]

C

candidates (kan′də dāts′) people who try to win an office or honor [5]

cargo (kär′gō) goods carried by a ship, plane, or other vehicle [20]

ceremonies (ser′ə mō′nēz) traditional events that follow a pattern or set of rules [15]

classes (klas′əz) groups of people who have the same importance in society [9]

climate (klī′mit) the usual weather patterns for an area over time [4]

colonies (kol′ə nēz) lands that are under the control of another country [9]

compete (kəm pēt′) to work against others to win a contest or prize [17]

***conclusion** (kən kloo͞′zhən) a final decision or opinion [4]

***confined** (kən fīnd′) held within a location [12]

***conflict** (kon′flikt) disagreement [6]

confusion (kən fū′zhən) the state of having disordered or mixed ideas or thoughts [9]

***consisted** (kən sist′əd) was made up of [16]

consumer (kən soo͞′mər) someone who buys or uses a product [14]

***contact** (kon′takt) the act of two things touching [7]

***contemporary** (kən tem′pə rer′ē) current; modern [10]

***contracted** (kən trak′tid) became affected by [12]

controversy (kon′trə vur′sē) a disagreement that involves different opinions [5]

conveys (kən vāz′) expresses; communicates [13]

councils (koun′səlz) groups of people that citizens elect to make decisions and laws for a city [14]

critics (krit′iks) people who disapprove of or find fault with something [5]

***currency** (kur′ən sē) money that people currently use [17]

customs (kus′təmz) social traditions of a group of people [10]

D

damaged (dam′ijd) hurt; made less valuable or useful [20]

debris (də brē′) bits of rock or other material that have been broken up and scattered [4]

defeated (di fēt′əd) having lost a competition or battle; beaten [7]

defendants (di fen′dənts) people who go on trial before a judge because they may have broken a law [13]

desperately (des′prit lē) deeply and hopelessly [11]

despite (di spīt′) not prevented by something [12]

***devoted** (di vō′tid) committed to some purpose [2]

dialogue (dī′ə lôg′) conversation, or words spoken, between people in a story [10]

***dispose** (dis pōz′) to throw away [2]

divine (di vīn′) heavenly; godlike [3]

domesticate (də mes′tə kāt′) to change animals or plants from a wild state to a controlled state [18]

* Academic English word

Lesson numbers appear in brackets.

E

efficiently (i fish′ənt lē) with as little effort or waste as possible [14]

elaborate (i lab′ər it) very detailed or complicated [2]

elite (i lēt′) best; most select [9]

emblem (em′bləm) an object or picture that represents another object or an idea [17]

***encounter** (en koun′tər) to face or experience something difficult [10]

engineers (en′ji nērz′) people trained to design, build, or use machines or structures [20]

***environment** (en vī′rən mənt) all things that may affect the ability of people, animals, and plants to survive and grow [14]

erosion (i rō′zhən) the process in which wind or water slowly wears down or washes away soil and rock [8]

exchange (iks chānj′) to give an item or service in return for something of equal value [16]

excursions (iks kur′zhənz) short trips that people take for fun or for a specific purpose [2]

executive (ig zek′yə tiv) a person who directs or manages a company or a government [14]

extends (iks tendz′) continues in a certain direction for a certain distance [18]

extinct (iks tingkt′) no longer in existence [4]

F

Fertile Crescent (furt′əl kres′ənt) a curved strip of land between the Mediterranean Sea and the Persian Gulf [18]

festivals (fes′tə vəlz) feasts, parties, or holidays that mark a special event [2]

flourish (flur′ish) to grow or develop very successfully [18]

***foundations** (foun dā′shənz) the lowest parts of a structure that support the other parts [3]

***functions** (fungk′shənz) operates; works [14]

G

grease (grēs) a thick, oily liquid that makes materials more slippery or smooth [15]

Great Depression (grāt di presh′ən) the period in U.S. history from 1929 to 1941, when the economy was poor and many people lost their jobs [12]

guilty (gil′tē) responsible for a wrong action that deserves punishment [13]

H

harvest (här′vist) the time when people gather crops that are ready to be eaten [2]

historical (his tôr′i kəl) involving past events or people [10]

I

***impact** (im′pakt) a strong effect [4]

***implement** (im′plə ment′) to begin to use something [18]

***incorporate** (in kôr′pə rāt′) to include as a part [9]

***indicates** (in′di kāts′) shows [3]

infamous (in′fə məs) widely known for bad things [11]

insurance (in shoor′əns) protection against risk or loss; a contract that arranges for a person to pay money in exchange for a company's promise to pay money in the case of problems, such as illness or property damage [12]

intense (in tens′) very strong [1]

K

keen (kēn) sharp of mind; able to notice many details [18]

L

launched (lôncht) pushed or put into motion—especially into the air [8]

***legal** (lē′gəl) established or allowed by law [17]

legend (lej′ənd) a traditional story that many people believe to be true [11]

longevity (lon jev′ə tē) length of life or existence [3]

lured (loord) created a powerful interest; attracted [9]

M

***minority** (mə nôr′ə tē) a racial, religious, political, or other group that is different from the larger group it is a part of [5]

missions (mish′ənz) specific tasks that groups of people accomplish [8]

motto (mot′ō) a short phrase that states an idea or a belief [3]

N

novels (nov′əlz) long works of fiction that tell stories with characters [10]

* Academic English word

Lesson numbers appear in brackets.

O

***objective** (əb jek′tiv) a goal or result that someone works toward [19]

obstacles (ob′stə kəlz) things that stand in the way or make something more difficult [19]

***occurred** (ə kurd′) took place [18]

opponents (ə pō′nənts) people who work against each other, such as in a game [19]

origin (ôr′ə jin) the source that something comes from [1]

P

pastime (pas′tīm′) an activity that helps people pass time in a pleasant way [19]

penalty (pen′əl tē) a punishment for breaking a law or a rule [7]

peninsula (pə nin′sə lə) an area of land that sticks out from the mainland and is almost completely surrounded by water [4]

plot (plot) the main story of a book, movie, play, or poem [10]

***positive** (poz′ə tiv) helpful; good [5]

potent (pōt′ənt) strong; powerful [13]

poverty (pov′ər tē) lack of money or possessions [12]

***precise** (pri sīs′) very exact [8]

present (prez′ənt) in a particular place at a certain time [13]

presented (pri zent′əd) produced [16]

***prime** (prīm) first in rank or importance [15]

***promote** (prə mōt′) to try to sell something or make people like something [13]

propel (prə pel′) to cause something to move forward [7]

***publish** (pub′lish) to put into printed form to give or sell to the public [13]

R

resembles (ri zem′bəlz) looks like; is similar to [17]

***response** (ri spons′) an action that occurs because of another action; a reaction [1]

***retained** (ri tānd′) continued to have or hold [6]

revival (ri vī′vəl) the act of something coming back into existence or use [6]

revolted (ri vōlt′əd) rose up against a government or ruling body [11]

***revolution** (rev′ə lo͞o′shən) an event that occurs when people fight against an existing government to replace it with a new one [11]

rhythm (rith′əm) a pattern of sounds that repeat in an orderly way [1]

***rigid** (rij′id) strict; not willing or able to change [11]

rituals (rich′o͞o əlz) religious or serious ceremonies that follow set rules and patterns [2]

role (rōl) a part that someone or something plays [15]

rumors (ro͞o′mərz) stories that people tell whether or not they are true [6]

S

sacred (sā′krid) worthy of religious respect [15]

satellite (sat′əl īt′) an object that travels around a body in space, such as Earth [8]

seal (sēl) an official stamp or design of a person, group, or government [3]

***significant** (sig nif′i kənt) large in amount or quantity [20]

slaughtered (slô′tərd) killed an animal for food [16]

sponsor (spon′sər) a person or group that pays for an event or a program [5]

starved (stärvd) died from hunger [16]

stereotype (ster′ē ə tīp′) to present a person or group in an overly simple way based on how people believe that person or group usually acts [5]

stock (stok) part ownership of a company, which people can buy and sell [12]

strokes (strōks) movements, such as hits, that people do with tools [19]

T

***target** (tär′git) an object or a mark to aim for [19]

***technology** (tek nol′ə jē) methods and devices that help expand scientific knowledge in a certain field of study [8]

tended (tend′əd) cared for; watched over [16]

thrived (thrīvd) existed very successfully [4]

treaty (trē′tē) an agreement signed by two or more countries or other groups [17]

turmoil (tur′moil) confusion that creates unrest [6]

U

***undergo** (un′dər gō′) to pass through [9]

union (ūn′yən) a group that joins together for a common purpose [17]

V

vital (vīt′əl) necessary for life [15]

vulgar (vul′gər) in poor taste; with bad manners [7]

W

wailed (wāld) made a long sound like a cry of sadness or pain [1]

* Academic English word

Lesson numbers appear in brackets.